Hiker's & Biker's Guide to Cook County, Illinois

An American Bike Trails Publication

Hiker's & Biker's Guide to Cook County, Illinois

Published by	American Bike Trails
Copyright 2006 by	American Bike Trails
Created by	Ray Hoven
Illustrated & Designed by	Mary C. Rumpsa

Cover photo courtesy of The Chicago Botanic Garden

Table of Contents

Table of Contents (continued)

Acknowledgements

We greatly appreciate the support, input, and guidance provided by the many professionals who contributed to the development of this book:

John Carlson	Village of Barlett
Dave Kircher	Forest Preserve District of Cook County
Ana Koval	I&M Canal Corridor Association
Julie McCaffrey	Chicago Botanic Garden
Claudia Regoto	North Park Village
Bob Sullivan	Village of Orland Park, Dept. of Parks
Dan White	Forest Preserve District of Cook County
Ron Vasile	I&M Canal Corridor Association
Spring Valley Nature Center	Schaumburg Park District

Definition of Terms

Natural Community An indigenous group of organisms – interrelated with each other and their environment. Natural communities may be defined at any scale, from biome to micro association. Important characteristics include soil moisture, substrate, soil reaction, species composition, vegetation structure, and topographic position.

Prairie Grassland community in full sun dominated by a matrix of perennial grasses and supporting a diversity of forbs which forms a dry flammable turf. Prairies are essentially treeless, but shrubs may be present. Types range from wet to dry and include gravel hill, sand, dolomite bedrock and black soil prairies. Illinois is in the Tallgrass Prairie region.

Savanna Any area where scattered trees and/or shrubs occur over a continuous and permanent groundlayer, usually dominated by herbs. Savannas, considered fire-dependent grassland communities, range from dry (black oak savannas) to wet (swamp white oak savannas).

Woodland Community dominated in by a mix of oaks with understory trees. Moderately dense trees and shrubs (25-80% canopy) occurring over a continuous and permanent herbaceous groundlayer. A fire-dependent community which burned regularly if infrequently.

Forest Community dominated by maple with a dense canopy, more than 60-80%, and an understory vegetation not dominated by grasses. Characterized by multiple layers of shrubs, understory trees and canopy trees; shade tolerant herbaceous plants form the ground layer. In our area forests occur east of Lake Michigan and in ravines, floodplains and on the east side of large rivers. Forests are not fire-dependent communities although fires occasionally occurred.

Wetland   Community or system having soils that are saturated, flooded or ponded long enough during the growing season to develop anaerobic conditions that favor the growth of hydrophytic vegetation (growing partially or wholly immersed in water). Wetlands include bogs, fens, marshes, swamps, interdunal swales, wet prairies, sedge meadows and woodland ponds.

Shrub   Brushwood. A low, usually several-stemmed, woody plant.

Herb   A seed producing annual, biennial, or perennial that does not develop persistent woody tissue but dies down at the end of a growing season.

Bog   Wet, spongy ground. A poorly drained usually acid area rich in plant residues, frequently surrounding a body of open water, and have a characteristic flora.

Fen   Low land covered wholly or partly with water unless artificially drained.

Marsh   A tract of soft wet land usually characterized by monocotyledons, such as grass or cattails.

Swale   A lower lying or depressed and often wet stretch of land.

Sedge   Turfed marsh plant having achene's and solid stems.

Health Hazards

Hypothermia

Hypothermia is a condition where the core body temperature falls below 90 degrees. This may cause death.

Mild hypothermia
- 1. Symptoms
  - a. Pronounced shivering
  - b. Loss of physical coordination
  - c. Thinking becomes cloudy
- 2. Causes
  - a. Cold, wet, loss of body heat, wind
- 3. Treatment
  - a. Prevent further heat loss, get out of wet clothing and out of wind. Replace wet clothing with dry.
  - b. Help body generate more heat. Refuel with high-energy foods and a hot drink, get moving around, light exercise, or external heat.

Severe hypothermia
- 1. Symptoms
  - a. Shivering stops, pulse and respiration slows down, speech becomes incoherent.
- 2. Treatment
  - a. Get help immediately.
  - b. Don't give food or water.
  - c. Don't try to rewarm the victim in the field.
  - d. A buildup of toxic wastes and tactic acid accumulates in the blood in the body's extremities. Movement or rough handling will cause a flow of the blood from the extremities to the heart. This polluted blood can send the heart into ventricular fibrillations (heart attack). This may result in death.
  - e. Wrap victim in several sleeping bags and insulate from the ground.

Frostbite

Symptoms of frostbite may include red skin with white blotches due to lack of circulation. Rewarm body parts gently. Do not immerse in hot water or rub to restore circulation, as both will destroy skin cell.

Heat Exhaustion

Cool, pale, and moist skin, heavy sweating, headache, nausea, dizziness and vomiting. Body temperature nearly normal.

Treatment	Have victim lie in the coolest place available– on back with feet raised. Rub body gently with cool, wet cloth. Give person ½ glass of water every 15 minutes if conscious and can tolerate it. Call for emergency medical assistance.

Heat Stroke

Hot, red skin, shock or unconsciousness; high body temperature.

Treatment	Treat as a life-threatening emergency. Call for emergency medical assistance immediately. Cool victim by any means possible. Cool bath, pour cool water over body, or wrap wet sheets around body. Give nothing by mouth.

West Nile Virus

West Nile Virus is transmitted by certain types of mosquitoes. Most people infected with West Nile Virus won't develop symptoms. Some may become ill 3 to 15 days after being bitten.

Protect Yourself	Wear proper clothing, use insect repellents and time your outdoor activities to reduce your risk of mosquito bites and other insect problems. Most backyard mosquito problems are caused by mosquitoes breeding in and around homes, not those from more natural areas.

Tips for Bicyclists

Pushing in gears that are too high can push knees beyond their limits. Avoid extremes by pedaling faster rather than shifting into a higher gear.

Keeping your elbows bent, changing your hand position frequently and wearing bicycle gloves all help to reduce the numbness or pain in the palm of the hand from long-distance riding.

Keep you pedal rpms up on an uphill so you have reserve power if you lose speed.

Stay in a high-gear on a level surface, placing pressure on the pedals and resting on the handle bars and saddle.

Lower your center of gravity on a long or steep downhill run by using the quick release seat post binder and dropping the saddle height down.

Brake intermittently on a rough surface.

Wear proper equipment. Wear a helmet that is approved by the Snell Memorial Foundation or the American National Standards Institute. Look for one of their stickers inside the helmet.

Use a lower tire inflation pressure for riding on unpaved surfaces. The lower pressure will provide better tire traction and a more comfortable ride.

Apply your brakes gradually to maintain control on loose gravel or soil.

Ride only on trails designated for bicycles or in areas where you have the permission of the landowner.

Be courteous to hikers or horseback riders on the trail, they have the right of way.

Leave riding trails in the condition you found them. Be sensitive to the environment. Properly dispose of your trash. If you open a gate, close it behind you.

Don't carry items or attach anything to your bicycle that might hinder your vision or control.

Don't wear anything that restricts your hearing.

Don't carry extra clothing where it can hang down and jam in a wheel.

Trail Rules

Leave nature as you find it for others to enjoy.

Do not collect or remove any natural objects.

Deposit litter in proper receptacles

Stay on trails

Be alert for cars or bicycles

Don't feed the wildlife.

Check for ticks when you're finished.

Don't wear earphones. You can't hear a bicyclist coming.

Relax, have fun, and enjoy!

Specifics for Bicyclists

Wear a helmet.

Ride in single file.

Be alert for loose gravel, debris, holes, or bumps on the trails.

Keep both hands on your handlebars.

Apply your brakes gradually to maintain control on loose gravel or soil.

Cautiously pass hikers on the left. Call out "passing on the left".

Be courteous to hikers or horseback riders on the trail. They have the right of way.

Don't carry items or attach anything to your bicycle that might hinder your vision or control.

Don't carry extra clothing where it can hang down and jam in a wheel.

Trail Statistics

Park, Preserve or Trail	Miles Hike	Miles Bike	Surface
Algonquin Road Trail	9.5	9.5	Asphalt
Arie Crown Bicycle Trail	3.2	3.2	Crushed Gravel
Bemis Woods	3.0	3.0	Packed earth
Black Partridge Forest Preserve	0.5		Packed earth
Busse Woods Forest Preserve Trail	11.2	11.2	Asphalt
Centennial Trail (partially complete)	20.0	20.0	Crushed stone
Chicago Botanic Garden	7.0		Paved, woodchips
Chicago Lakefront Bike Path	20.0	20.0	Asphalt
Cook County I&M Canal Trail	8.9	8.9	Paved
Crabtree Nature Center	3.3		Woodchips, packed earth
Deer Grove Forest Preserve Trail	12.3	12.3	Asphalt, gravel, packed earth
Des Plaines Division	10.0	10.0	Natural, groomed
Des Plaines River Trail & Greenway	33.0	33.0	Limestone screenings
Evanston Bikeways	7.0	7.0	Asphalt
Grand Illinois Trail	475.0	475.0	Asphalt, screenings, streets
Green Bay Trail	6.0	6.0	Asphalt
I&M Canal National HC	61.5	61.5	Limestone screenings
Illinois Prairie Path	55.0	55.0	Limestone screenings, some paved
Indian Boundary Division	10.8	10.8	Natural, groomed

Park, Preserve or Trail	Miles		Surface
	Hike	Bike	
John Humphrey Bike Trail	4.0	4.0	Paved
Lake Katherine Nature Preserve	3.5		Woodchips, mowed turf
Lemont's I&M Canal Trail	6.8	6.8	Crushed limestone
North Branch Bicycle Trail	20.0	20.0	Asphalt
North Park Village Nature Center	2.5		Woodchip
Old Plank Road Trail	21.0	21.0	Asphalt
Palatine Trails & Bikeways	15.0	15.0	Paved, connecting streets
Palos & Sag Forest Preserve Trails	32.0	32.0	Natural, groomed
Poplar Creek Trail	9.5	9.5	Asphalt
River Trail Nature Center	1.5		Groomed
Robert McClory Bike Path	25.0	25.0	Limestone screenings, paved
Salt Creek Forest Preserve Trail	6.6	6.6	Asphalt
Sand Ridge Nature Center	3.5		Packed dirt, boardwalk
Spring Creek Valley Forest Preserve	*		Groomed
Spring Valley Nature Sanctuary	3.0		Groomed
Thorn Creek Bicycle Trail	9.3	9.3	Asphalt
Tri-County Trail	*		Mowed Turf
Tinley Creek Forest Preserve Trail	23.5	23.5	Asphalt
Wolf Road Prairie	2.0		Paved, mowed turf

Length Undetermined

Explanation of Symbols

SYMBOL LEGEND

🏊	Beach/Swimming
🚲	Bicycle Repair
🏠	Cabin
▲	Camping
◢	Canoe Launch
+	First Aid
🍴	Food
GC	Golf Course
?	Information
🛏	Lodging
MF	Multi-Facilities
P	Parking
🎋	Picnic
🏃	Ranger Station
🚻	Restrooms
⌂	Shelter
T	Trailhead
🏛	Visitor Center
🚰	Water
👪	Overlook/Observation

AREA LEGEND

	City, Town
	Parks, Preserves
	Waterway
	Marsh/Wetland
▬▬▬	Mileage Scale
★	Points of Interest
– – –	County/State
🌲	Forest/Woods

TRAIL LEGEND

▬▬▬▬	Trail-Biking/Multi
············	Skiing only Trail
●●●●●●●●●	Hiking only Trail
=========	Planned Trail
▬ ▬ ▬ ▬	Alternate Trail
▬▬▬▬	Road/Highway
+++++++++	Railroad Tracks

Algonquin Road Trail &
Paul Douglas Forest Preserve

Trail Length	9.5 miles
Surface	Asphalt
Contact	Forest Preserve District of Cook County 708-366-9420

The Algonquin Trail is located in northwest Cook County. It runs from Harper College west to Pottawatomie Woods. The trail generally parallels Algonquin Road, but there is a 6 mile loop around the parameter of the Paul Douglas Forest Preserve and the Highland Woods Golf Course south of Algonquin Road. The setting is open and urban, with woods as you enter the Forest Preserve. Arlington Heights Road was once a Pottawatomie Indian trail, one of several in the area. The road was first paved in 1926, and its name changed from State Road in 1962. Harper College is a community college with an enrollment of about 15,000.

The Paul Douglas Forest Preserve is a 1,800 acre parcel of former cropland with large stretches of treeless territory for birds to breed in. Since the restoration of a large wetland near Poplar Creek, many open-wetland species can now also call the preserve home, including pied-billed grebes, ruddy ducks, and yellow-headed blackbirds. The preserve's main wetland with its heron rookery close to the parking lot makes it a convenient and popular spot to see these wetland birds. Those who want more immersion should head northwest of the main wetland, to one of the preserve's larger grasslands to observe bobolinks, eastern meadowlarks, savannah sparrows and other species that nest in the grasses and goldenrod.

Getting There   A good place to kick off your west bound Algonquin Road Trail ride is from one of the many parking lots at Harper College. It's also an excellent opportunity to visit the college campus, especially by taking a tour of their outdoor sculptures. The western trailhead is located at the entrance to Pottawatomie Woods at Palatine and Strover Roads.

The entrance to the Paul Douglas Forest Preserve is located off Central Road east of Freeman Road and west of Ela Road.

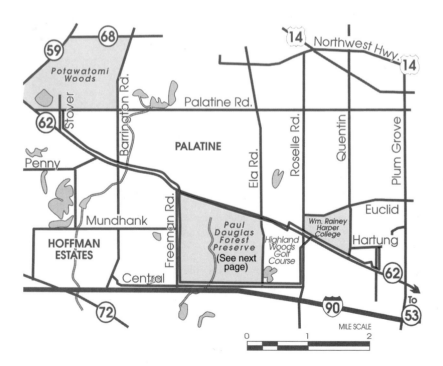

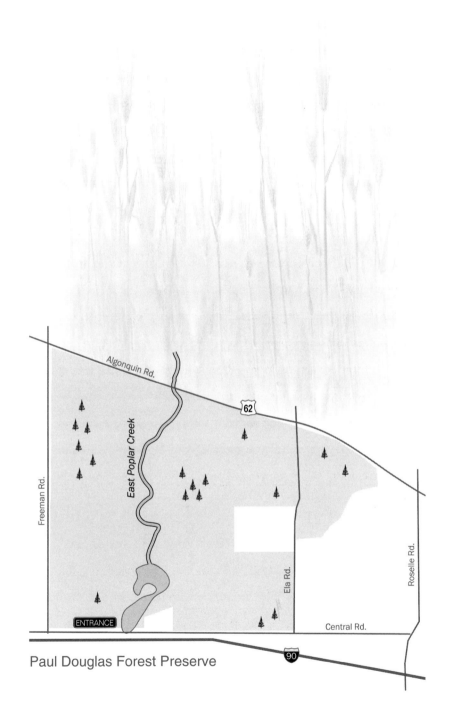

Paul Douglas Forest Preserve

Arie Crown Forest Preserve and Trail

Trail Length	3.2 miles
Surface	Crushed gravel
Contact	Forest Preserve District of Cook County 708-366-9420
County	Cook

The Arie Crown Trail offers you a natural setting of gently rolling hills as it winds through the scenic Arie Crown Forest near Hodgkins. Wildflowers and many other native plants adorn the trail's edge, making it one of the more beautiful in the area. The trail is open from sunrise to sunset. There are several loops and trail intersections, so it is easy to get lost. There are also a few hills to climb, a small creek to cross, and nearby Lake Ida to enjoy. The northern portion is quiet and peaceful, but traffic sounds increase as you approach I-55 to the south. Facilities include restrooms, water pumps, and picnic tables near several of the parking areas.

Getting There   The Arie Crown Forest Preserve is located just northwest of the Cook County I&M Canal near Countryside and the Stevenson Expressway (I-55). The preserve can be accessed at Brainard and Joliet Road or LaGrange/Mannheim Road, north of 67th Street.

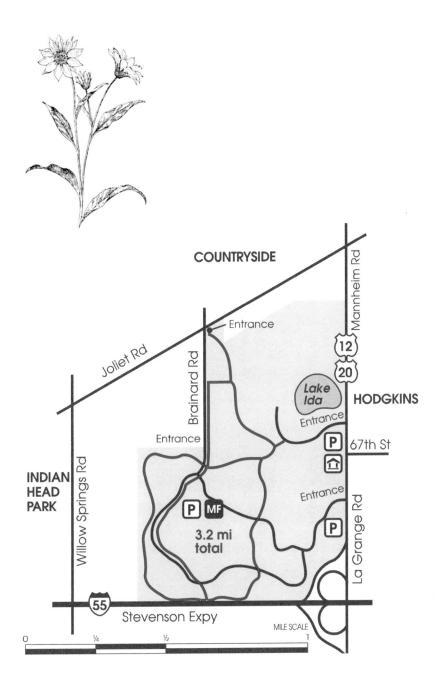

COUNTRYSIDE

Mannheim Rd

Joliet Rd

Brainard Rd

Entrance

12
20

Lake
Ida

HODGKINS

Entrance

Entrance

P 67th St

INDIAN
HEAD
PARK

Willow Springs Rd

P MF

3.2 mi
total

Entrance

P

La Grange Rd

55 Stevenson Expy

MILE SCALE

0   ¼   ½   1

Bemis Woods

Trail Length	3 miles
Surface	Packed earth
Contact	Forest Preserve District of Cook County 708-771-1330
County	Cook

This a is 3 mile unpaved, multi-use trail running through the gently rolling terrain by Salt Creek in Bemis Woods Preserve north of Western Springs. The western trailhead for the Salt Creek Bicycle Trail is also here. The trail loops through hilly woodland and along the meandering creek. The surface is packed earth with loose gravel in some spots. The path is mostly 8 to 10 feet wide but narrows to a single track overgrown with vegetation in some spots. It's easy to lose your way with all the trail intersections. Bemis Woods is open to hikers, bicyclists and equestrians.

Getting There   Take Ogden Avenue (Route 34) .5 miles east of I-294. The entrance is to the north. There is a second entrance a bit farther east off of Wolf Road .6 miles north of Ogden. Both entrances provide easy access to the multi-use trail.

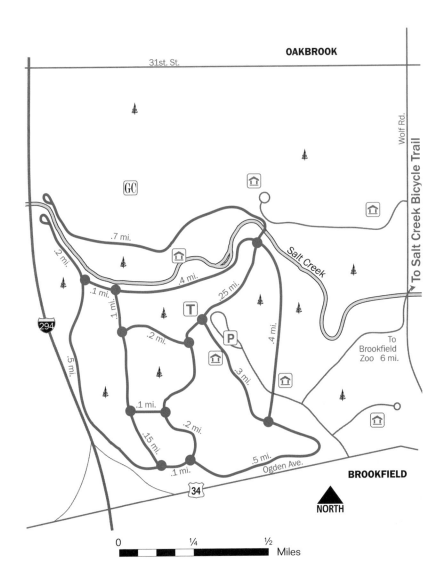

OAKBROOK

31st. St.

Wolf Rd.

To Salt Creek Bicycle Trail

GC

Salt Creek

.7 mi.

.2 mi.

.1 mi.

.1 mi.

.4 mi.

.25 mi.

T

P

.2 mi.

.4 mi.

.3 mi.

.5 mi.

.1 mi.

.15 mi.

.2 mi.

.1 mi.

.5 mi.

294

To
Brookfield
Zoo 6 mi.

Ogden Ave.

BROOKFIELD

NORTH

34

0   ¼   ½
                        Miles

Black Partridge Forest Preserve

Trail Length	0.5 mile
Surface	Packed earth
Contact	Forest Preserve District of Cook County 708-771-1330
County	Cook

Named for the Pottawatomie Indian chief Black Partridge, this 80 acre preserve was dedicated in 1965 to protect its spring-fed system. A dense tree canopy, interspersed with several small clearings, covers the majority of the preserve. The trails at Black Partridge are challenging with many steep and winding ravines. It borders the Sanitary Drainage and Ship Canal on the north. The mesic forest are dominated by sugar maple, basswood, red oak, and white oak, while the seep springs support skunk cabbage, marsh marigold, and a wide variety of wildflowers. Common animal species in the preserve include woodcock, gray squirrel, wood pewee, and redheaded woodpecker.

Getting There   From I-55, exit at Lemont Road. Proceed south on Lemont Road to 111th Street (Bluff Road), then left (west) for one mile. The preserve is on the right.

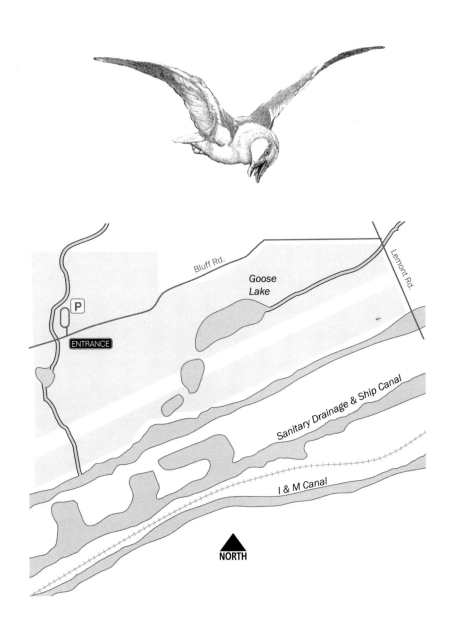

Bluff Rd.

Goose
Lake

Lemont Rd.

P

ENTRANCE

Sanitary Drainage & Ship Canal

I & M Canal

NORTH

Busse Woods Bicycle Trail

Trail Length   11.2 miles

Surface   Asphalt paved

Contact   Forest Preserve District of Cook County
708-366-9420

This 11.2 mile paved asphalt trail meanders through woods and around the 590 acre Busse Lake at the 3,700 acre Ned Brown Preserve. The preserve is located in northwest Cook County, bordered on the north by Arlington Heights and to the east by Elk Grove Village. The 427 acre Busse Forest is a registered national landmark and nature preserve due to its rich variety of upland and lowland native tree species. The preserve hosts over 2.5 million visits a year. It bustles with activity from the noticeable fishermen, boaters, bicyclers, and hikers, to the less obvious wildlife, but you still can find a place for solitude in this huge preserve.

A great place to hike is the Busse Forest nature trail in the northeastern part of the preserve. The pathway meanders through an oak, sugar maple and basswood forest. Partially packed-earth and sometimes gravel surfaced, the 2 miles of narrow footpath takes you through the nature preserve. Here the sounds of birds and insects drown out the traffic noise. If you are looking for a peaceful, quiet walk in beautiful woods, you will enjoy Busse Forest. The nature trails are only open to hiking.

The aquatic vegetation in the shallows and drop-off areas of the lake provide perfect habitat for northern pike, bullhead, crappie, and other fish. Many species of migrating ducks as well as shorebirds such as yellowleg seek the shallows to dine on succulent lake greens to fatten themselves up in spring or fall before continuing their journey. Filled with oak, basswood, and maple trees, the wooded areas provide cooling respite for hikers and bicyclists on a warm summer day. White oak and basswood thrive in the dryer uplands while swamp white oaks and ashes grow well in the wetter lowlands. In spring, the woods burst with spring wildflowers such as great white trillium and wild geranium, catching the sun's ray before the trees leaves unfurl and block the light.

While you can enter the bike path at many different locations, this tour will start at Bisner Road on the south side. The path runs north of and parallel to the Bisner Road entrance parking areas. In addition to the 7.8 mile loop, there are several spurs out to communities along the way. Park in the first section available, and head right on the pathway. Turn left (north) at the first trail intersection. The trail crosses over the south pool of the lake and runs by the Busse Lake boating center. Here you can rent a boat, or pause at the refreshment stand (open in warm weather). The lake meanders through the preserve with small islands in several spots. The path continues north and crosses Higgins Road at a stoplight and a push-to-cross button. To cover the entire route turn left at the trail intersection north of Higgins. The path leads through the Ned Brown Meadow and near a model airplane field, then turns east along Golf Road crossing over Salt Creek where it enters the preserve. Here the off-road trail ends near an I-90 underpass. An on-road Arlington Heights bike route starts at Wilke Road heading north.

To continue on the forest preserve bicycle trail, turn back and return to the trail intersection north of Higgins Road. Take the path to the left heading southeast along Higgins. The path will enter Busse Forest and head northeast. Here the previously relative flat terrain becomes a long

Busse Woods Bicycle Trail (continued)

gradual climb before turning south with a long descent. The path will skirt around a fence enclosing a 14 acre pasture, where a number of captive elk reside today. A couple of hundred years ago their ancestors roamed free in this area. Past the enclosure, you'll come to a bridge providing safe crossing over busy Higgins Road.

After a short distance through an open meadow, the path re-enters the woods for a bit heading south. Continue through the parking area as the trail turns back west. Stay on the path to the right to return to the Bisner Road parking area. From this starting point the pathway continues south another .9 mile along Bisner to Biesterfield Road. Water pumps, picnic tables, and restrooms can be found at all the parking areas.

Getting There   Parking is available near the bike path at the following locations: on Golf Road .2 mile east of Route 53, on Arlington Heights Road north of Higgins, and another location south of Landmeier Road. Parking is also available at four locations on Higgins between Arlington Heights Road and Route 53. On the south side take Biesterfield Road east to Bisner Road then north on Bisner to the entrance on the left. If you're biking to the preserve, take the Schaumburg Bikeways east along Woodfield Road. From the Arlington Heights Bikeways, take the Wilke Road route south to Golf Road.

To get to the Busse Forest nature trail, take the eastern-most entrance road off Higgins Road for 1 mile to the parking area on the east side of the road. The trail entrance is across the road north of an Illinois Nature Preserve sign.

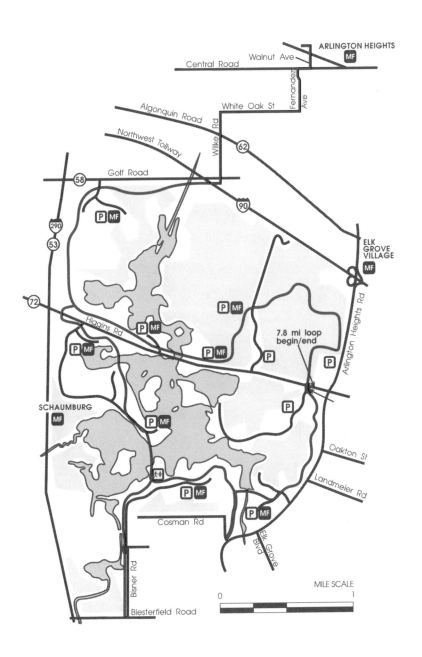

ARLINGTON HEIGHTS
MF

Central Road

Walnut Ave

Fernandez Ave

White Oak St

Algonquin Road

Wilke Rd

Northwest Tollway

62

58

Golf Road

290

53

P MF

ELK GROVE VILLAGE
MF

72

Higgins Rd

P MF

P MF

P MF

P MF

Arlington Heights Rd

7.8 mi loop begin/end

P

P

SCHAUMBURG
MF

P MF

P

Oakton St

Landmeier Rd

P MF

Cosman Rd

P MF

Elk Grove Blvd

90

Bisner Rd

Biesterfield Road

MILE SCALE

0   1

Camp Sagawau

Trail Length	Undetermined
Surface	Natural
Contact	Camp Sagawau 630-257-2045

Camp Sagawau is a 12 acre preserve located in southwest Cook County south of the Cal-Sag Channel near Lemont. It is a protected site, due to the unusual number of rare and threatened species in need of preservation found here, and is only open for scheduled programs. Special programs include naturalist guided walks, field trips, and environmental education workshops. The nature center offers more than 70 different naturalist-led nature education programs throughout the year.

Its primary attraction is the only exposed canyon of its kind in Cook County. Formed of the region's bedrock dolomite limestone, the canyon provides a distinctive environment for wildlife. In spring, lush green ferns begin to unfold from closed fiddle-like branches to lacy green delights. Naturalists will also lead you on fossil hunts and in the winter, you can participate in Nordic ski clinics. The camp is open for cross-country skiing when the snow base is sufficient.

Getting There   Take I-55 South and exit on 83 South (Kingery Road). Proceed south to 111th Street, and then turn left and go a short distance to the camp entrance on the left.

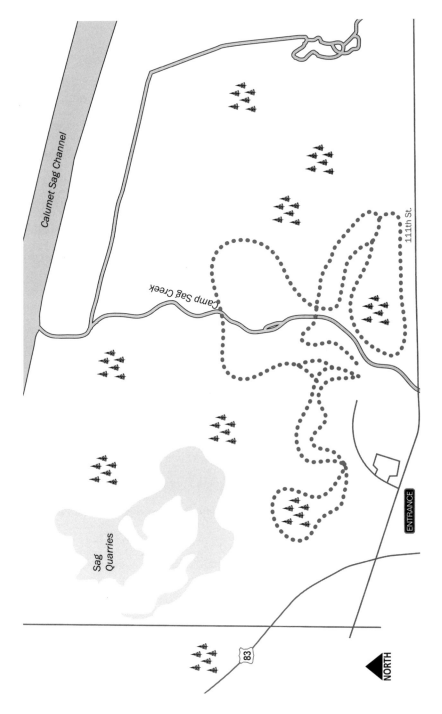

Calumet Sag Channel

Camp Sag Creek

111th St.

Sag Quarries

ENTRANCE

83

NORTH

Centennial Trail (under development)

Trail Length	20 miles
Surface	Crushed stone
Contact	Forest Preserve District of Will County 815-727-8700
Counties	Will, Cook, DuPage

This planned 20 mile trail will run from the Chicago Portage site at Lyons in Cook County to Lockport in Will County. It forms a link in the Grand Illinois Trail. The setting is suburban with most services readily available.

For an interesting side hike, visit the Ottawa Trail Woods Preserve and the Chicago Portage Woods in Lyons. This is where Jolliet and Marquette discovered a connection between the Great Lakes and the Mississippi River. To get there take Harlem Avenue south of Joliet Road to the first entrance to the west for Ottawa Trail Woods Preserve. A little farther south on Harlem is the Chicago Portage Woods parking area. At Chicago Portage Woods is a National Historic Site honoring Marquette and Jolliet. A short footpath to the south takes you to portage Creek, and another to the west takes you to the Des Plaines River. In Ottawa Trail Woods, there is a footpath along the river leading to Laughton's Ford. Some two hundred years ago, Indian trails radiated out from this focal point.

From the portage site, the Centennial Trail will run on the north side of the Des Plaines River south to Willow Springs Road, then on a bridge crossing over the river. It then continues southwest between the river and the Chicago Sanitary & Ship Canal parallel to the Cook County I&M Canal Bicycle Trail. Southeast is the Palos Preserves. West of Palos, the Centennial Trail enters DuPage County near the Waterfall Glen Forest Preserve, continuing southwest through Lemont and connecting to Lemont's canal trail.

In Will County, a 3 mile section of the Centennial Trail is open from the Cook/Will County line to 135th Street in Romeoville near the Isle a la Cache Museum.

Getting There The northern trailhead will be located at the Chicago Portage National Historic Site in Lyons. Take Harlem Avenue south of Ogden Avenue and Joliet Avenue to 47th Street in Lyons. The entrance will be to the west. The southern trailhead is at 2nd Street in Lockport where it connects with the existing Gaylord Donnelley Canal Trail.

Chicago Botanic Garden

Pathways	7 miles
Surface	Paved, woodchips
Contact	Chicago Botanic Garden 847-835-8213

The Chicago Botanic Garden, a living museum of plants, is at Cook County's northern border. Here visitors can stroll through a serene Japanese garden, discover the six garden rooms of the English-walled Garden, experience the sensuous appeal of plants in the Sensory Garden, and explore 20 other gardens along 7 miles of pathways. Due to the great diversity of plants and habitats, bird life is plentiful here especially during migration. The 385 acre garden, owned by the Forest Preserve District of Cook County and managed by the Chicago Horticultural Society,

The English Walled Garden at the Chicago Botanic Garden

Photo courtesy of Chicago Botanic Garden

Evening Island at the Chicago Botanic Garden features vast sweeps of perennials in a tapestry of colors

Photo courtesy of Chicago Botanic Garden

contains over 2 million plants including trees and shrubs. If you visit the park on your bicycle, there are racks near the entrance to the visitor's center, where you can also pick up a copy of a visitor guide.

In the northeastern corner of the Garden is McDonalds Woods, a restored oak woodland community. The woodchip trail meanders through the woods. Secluded to the side, the nature trail is usually less crowded than the rest of the gardens. In the spring, wildflowers blanket the forest floor. The longest walk is the 15 acre prairie in the garden's south section. This prairie restoration has six different types of prairie communities: fen, gravel, hill, mesic (tall grass), sand, savanna, and wet. Interpretive signs explain prairie ecology.

The Botanic Garden serves as the trailhead for the 20 mile North Branch Bicycle Trail. One of the most scenic views in Chicagoland is on the service

Chicago Botanic Garden (continued)

road that serves as a bike route through the Garden from Dundee Road to Lake Cook Road. The lakes are visible for most of the route, but your favorite would probably be the Japanese Garden and in the background, the Waterfall Garden. Benches are nearby to sit and enjoy the view.

In the Visitor's Center, brochures provide information about the gardens. A restaurant is open for breakfast, lunch, and in the summer, dinner. Summer hours are from 7 am to 9 pm from June through August. From September through May, hours are from 8 am to sunset, everyday of the year except Christmas. Many programs are offered throughout the year. You can call 847-835-5440 for more information.

The Serpentine Bridge leads from the Sensory Garden to Evening Island

Photo courtesy of Chicago Botanic Garden

The Japanese Garden can be viewed from the bike path on the east side of the
Chicago Botanic Garden

Photo courtesy of Chicago Botanic Garden

Getting There   The main entrance is on Lake Cook Road (County
Line Road), .4 mile east of Route 41. There is a parking charge of $12.00
per vehicle. Admission is free. This provides a good incentive to hike or
bike! From the Green Bay Trail at the Braeside train station, you can bike
or walk on the sidewalk on the north side of Lake Cook Road .6 mile to
the main entrance where there is a stoplight for safe crossing. The Garden
can also be accessed from the south on bike or on foot through a walking
only entrance on Dundee Road just east of Route 41. This path is the
North Branch Bicycle Trail.

Chicago Botanic Garden (continued)

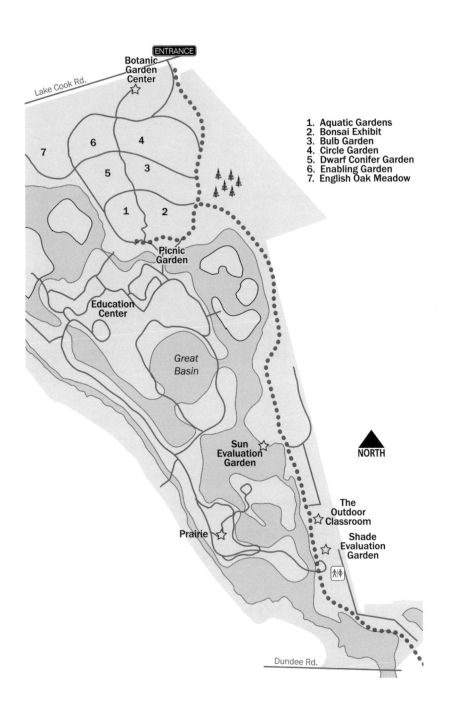

1. Aquatic Gardens
2. Bonsai Exhibit
3. Bulb Garden
4. Circle Garden
5. Dwarf Conifer Garden
6. Enabling Garden
7. English Oak Meadow

Chicago Lakefront Bike Path

Trail Length	Approximately 20 miles
Surface	Paved
Contact	Chicago Park District 312-747-2200
County	Cook

The symbolic starting point for a venture through the National Historic Corridor is Navy Pier in downtown Chicago. By bike or foot, you can arrive at the Pier by taking the Chicago Lakefront Bike Path. The Path offers great views of Lake Michigan and the Chicago Skyline. From the north, the bike path begins around Bryn Mawr (5600 north) and Sheridan Road, and then proceeds south along the shoreline to 71st Street. By motor vehicle take Lake Shore Drive, north of the loop to Illinois Street. Head east on Illinois Street to the parking area at Navy Pier. Restaurants, tour boats, and many other amusements await the visitor. Plenty of bike racks are available.

Navy Pier was built in 1926, and was envisioned as a recreational center for Chicagoans. The east end of the pier was the end of the line for the Grand Avenue streetcar. Navy Pier was named as a memorial to Midwesterners who served in the U.S. Navy in World War 1. Nearby points of interest include the Oak Street Beach, the Chicago Historical Society, and the Chicago Academy of Sciences to the north, and Buckingham Fountain, the Field Museum of Natural History, and Shedd Aquarium to the south.

Photo courtesy of Brook Collins/ Chicago Park District

When Fort Dearborn was built in 1803, the Chicago River flowed into Lake Michigan a short distance south of what today is Navy Pier. It was fed by northern and southern branches that converge at Wolf Point (near the Merchandise Mart) the river headed east for one mile along present day Wacker Drive. As Chicago grew, more and more raw sewage and pollutants were conveniently dumped in the river, which then transported the mess into Lake Michigan. Since Chicago water comes from Lake Michigan, its citizens received part of the polluted liquids back in the form of drinking water. In 1900, the problem was tackled by the opening of the 28 mile Chicago Sanitary and Ship Canal, which reversed the flow of the Chicago River. It begins at Damen Avenue and the Stevenson Expressway (I-55) in Chicago, and runs in a southwesterly direction through the suburbs of Stickney, Forest View, Lyons, Summit, Bedford, Park, Justice, Willow Springs, Lemont, and Romeoville. The canal terminates in Lockport, where it joins the Des Plaines River. The northern end of the canal joins the South Branch of the Chicago River. The average width of the channel is around 300 feet, and its 24-foot depth accommodates barge and other boat traffic.

The Friends of the Chicago River have produced a series of walking-tour brochures for the Chicago River Trail along or close to the waterway. Each brochure contains a map detailing a walking route for each section as well as historical information and item of interest along the river. You can call them at 312-939-0490 for more information about these walking tours and how to get the maps. Their web site is www.chicagoriver.org.

Chicago Lakefront Bike Path (continued)

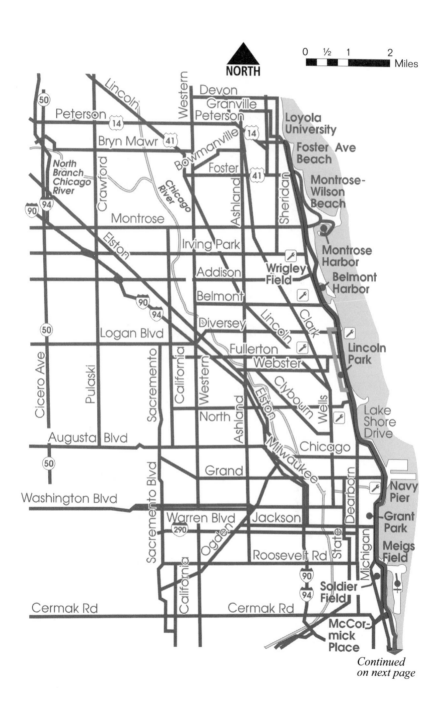

NORTH

0   ½   1   2 Miles

Lincoln
Devon
Western
Granville
Peterson
Peterson
14
50
14
Loyola University
Bryn Mawr
41
Bowmanville
Foster Ave Beach
North Branch Chicago River
Foster
41
Montrose-Wilson Beach
Crawford
Chicago River
Ashland
Sheridan
90
94
Montrose
Elston
Irving Park
Montrose Harbor
Addison
Wrigley Field
Belmont Harbor
Belmont
90
94
Diversey
Lincoln
Clark
Logan Blvd
50
Fullerton
Lincoln Park
Sacramento
California
Webster
Western
Clybourn
Pulaski
Cicero Ave
Ashland
Elston
Wells
Lake Shore Drive
North
Augusta Blvd
50
Chicago
Milwaukee
Sacremento Blvd
Grand
Dearborn
Navy Pier
Washington Blvd
Warren Blvd
Jackson
Grant Park
290
Ogden
State
Michigan
Meigs Field
Roosevelt Rd
California
90
94
Soldier Field
Cermak Rd
Cermak Rd
McCor-mick Place

Continued on next page

40

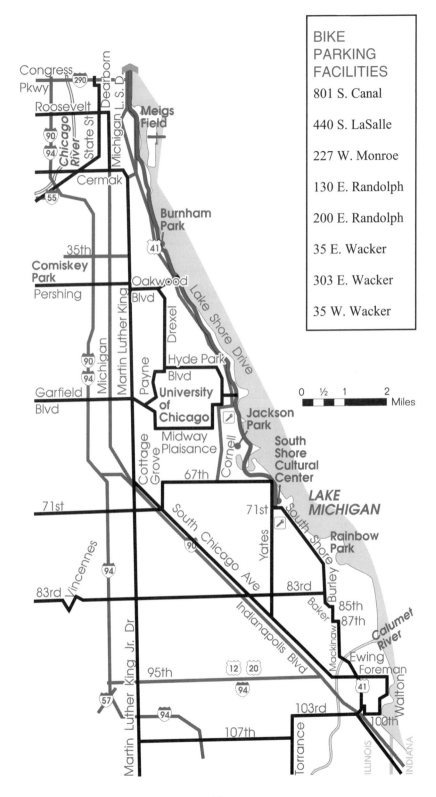

BIKE PARKING FACILITIES

801 S. Canal

440 S. LaSalle

227 W. Monroe

130 E. Randolph

200 E. Randolph

35 E. Wacker

303 E. Wacker

35 W. Wacker

Cook County I&M Bicycle Trail

Trail Length	8.9 miles
Surface	Paved
Contact	Palos Forest Preserve 708-361-1536
County	Cook

The paved I&M Canal Bicycle Trail is within the I&M Canal National Heritage Corridor. The 8.9 mile trail consists of three sections; two 3.3 mile loops and a 2.3 mile section that connects the two. From the parking area the trail heads northeast and southwest. Heading northeast, the asphalt trail leads through mature woods providing a shady and peaceful ride with little traffic sounds until you approach the I-194 underpass 1.6 miles out. Just past the interstate, the trail then heads back southwest paralleling the Chicago Sanitary and Ship Canal. Going southwest from the parking lot, you'll notice that soil and vegetation have filled in the canal. At the intersection 2.3 miles out from the parking lot trailhead is the other 3.3 mile loop along the canal. Taking the trail to the right takes you past two railroad crossings as well as a chemical company entrance. The trail ends at the Route 83 overpass and then loops back northeast.

Getting There   Take Route 83 south of the Des Plaines River to Archer Avenue, and then take Archer Avenue northwest of Willow Springs Road for 0.2 miles. Turn left on Market Street where you will see a large bicycle trail welcome sign. Continue for 0.2 miles through an industrial area. Cross under the Willow Springs Road bridge and over the Metra railroad tracks to the first parking lot.

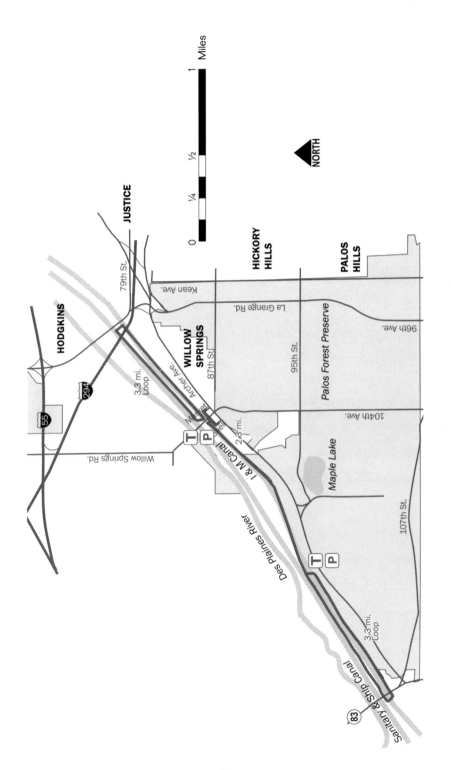

JUSTICE

HODGKINS

WILLOW
SPRINGS

HICKORY
HILLS

PALOS
HILLS

79th St.

Kean Ave.

La Grange Rd.

Archer Ave.

87th St.

95th St.

96th Ave.

104th Ave.

107th St.

Willow Springs Rd.

Market

Des Plaines River

I & M Canal

Palos Forest Preserve

Maple Lake

Sanitary & Ship Canal

3.3 mi.
Loop

2.3 mi.

3.3 mi.
Loop

NORTH

0   ¼   ½   1   Miles

Crabtree Nature Center

Trail Length	3.3 miles
Surface	Woodchip, packed earth
Contact	Forest Preserve District of Cook County
	708-366-8420

This 1,100 acre preserve was once farmland, but has been regenerated with forests, marshes, lakes, prairie and secondary growth, attracting many species of birds and countless flora and fauna. In spring and fall, migrating waterfowl rest here before continuing on their journeys. Bird watchers often set up their spotting scopes at a large lake along a trail to get closer looks of ruddy ducks, northern shovelers, bufflehead, and other colorful migratory waterfowl.

The nature trails here offers hikers opportunities to see and hear re-eyed vireos and scarlet tanagers in the woodlands and meadowlarks and bobolinks along the native prairie grasses such as a big blue stem and Indian grass. The 1.3 mile Bur Edge Nature Trail starts behind the exhibit building. The woodchip path loops around Sulky and Bullrush Ponds, through woods, and past Crabtree Lake. The 0.3 mile Great Hollow Trail forms a short loop off the nature trail near the exhibit building. On the east side of the Bur Edge Nature Trail, a 1.7 mile path leads to the Phantom Prairie. This 8 foot wide woodchip path allows easy access through this quiet, less-frequented area.

A drinking fountain, phone, and restrooms are available at the exhibit building. Nature programs are offered year-round including bird walks. Call 847-381-6592.

Getting There Take Palatine Road east of Algonquin Road and 1 mile west of Barrington Road. The entrance is to the north at Strover Road.

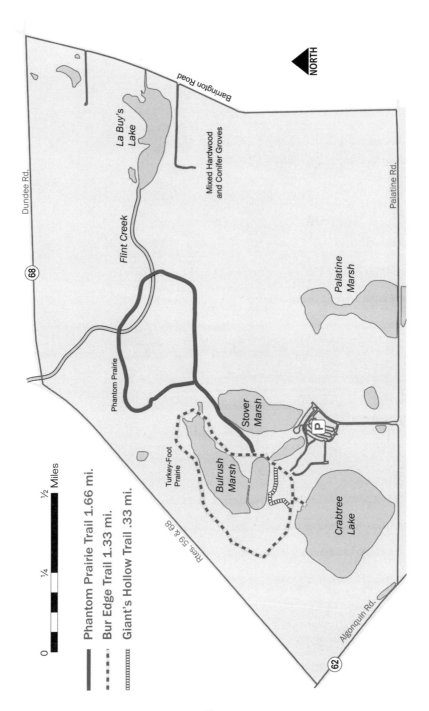

NORTH

La Buy's Lake

Barrington Road

Mixed Hardwood and Conifer Groves

Dundee Rd.

Palatine Rd.

Flint Creek

68

Palatine Marsh

Phantom Prairie

Stover Marsh

Turkey-Foot Prairie

Bulrush Marsh

P

Crabtree Lake

Rtes. 59 & 68

Algonquin Rd.

62

Phantom Prairie Trail 1.66 mi.

Bur Edge Trail 1.33 mi.

Giant's Hollow Trail .33 mi.

0   ¼   ½ Miles

Deer Grove Forest Preserve Trail

Trail Length	4 miles – leisure biking 8.3 miles - multi-use/mountain biking
Surface	Leisure – asphalt paved Multi-use – packed earth, gravel
Contact	Forest Preserve District of Cook County 708-366-9420

Deer Grove Preserve consists of rolling upland forest interspersed with wood ravines, and wetlands. Creeks meander through the tract, feeding two lakes located in the preserve. There is a 4 mile paved asphalt bicycle trail and 8.3 miles of unpaved, multi-use trail through the woodlands and meadows of this 1,800 acre preserve.

The asphalt bicycle path crosses the auto road near the first parking area of the easternmost entrance. Modern restrooms, a water pump, picnic tables, and shelters are available here. Heading east, the 10-foot wide bike trail runs through open fields and meadows with new growth trees nearby. After crossing over a creek, the trail turns north and loops back west along the creek. At some 2 miles out, a trail intersection offers two alternatives. The path left returns to the parking area completing a 2.8 mile loop. The path to the right leads to the central section of the preserve with mature woodland, hills and deep ravines. A ravine, a fragile ecosystem, hosts some unusual plant and animal life. Along the edges, you may notice the jewelweed growing, soft orange blooms in summer that attract hummingbirds. Heading west, the path climbs as you enter an oak and maple forest. Camp Reinberg is to your left. Quentin Road is the only road crossing. Be careful, as this is a busy highway.

The bike path is to the left. An auto road to the right leads to several parking areas farther in the woods. About a half mile west of the Quentin crossing, the bike path intersects with the auto road. Turn left and head up the hill on the auto road for 0.1 mile to pick up the continuation of the off-road bike path southeast of the parking area. The trail ends at the intersection of Quentin and Dundee Roads. You can connect here with the off-road segment of the Palatine Trail. Take the asphalt sidewalk on the southeastern corner of the intersection heading east for 0.2 mile and then south through the woods on the Palatine Trail. If you're not continuing on the Palatine Trail, you'll need to retrace your route back east.

white-tailed deer

Deer Grove Forest Preserve Trail (continued)

The 8.3 miles of multi-use trail at Deer Grove go through the forest and hilly terrain west of Quentin Road. The pathways range from single track to 10 foot wide with a packed-earth or gravel surface. Serving as hiking, equestrian, and cross-country ski trails, these unpaved, multi-use trails are bumpy and narrow in spots due to loose gravel, roots, and horse tracks. This is a good place for a quiet walk through the woods and along the lakes and marshes. Parts of the multi-use trail have been closed to bicycling at times due to the damage to ground cover plants and the resulting erosion of ravines. Restoration work days co-sponsored by the Forest Preserve District, environmental organizations, and trail use groups such a mountain bike advocates help with the recovery of damaged natural area.

In the winter, experienced cross-country skiers find the hills and curves on the Deer Grove trails challenging. Day-trippers will find water pumps, picnic tables, shelters and restrooms available at several picnic areas along the trail. The preserve is open from sunrise to sunset.

Getting There   Take Dundee Road west of Route 53 and Rand Road and east of Ela Road. There are three entrances off Dundee and one off Quentin Road, which bisects the preserve. If you plan to use the asphalt bike trail, the best place to park is the eastern entrance on Dundee, a half mile west of Hicks Rd. On bike or foot the Palatine Trail connects with the Deer Grove Bicycle Trail at the intersection of Dundee and Quentin Roads.

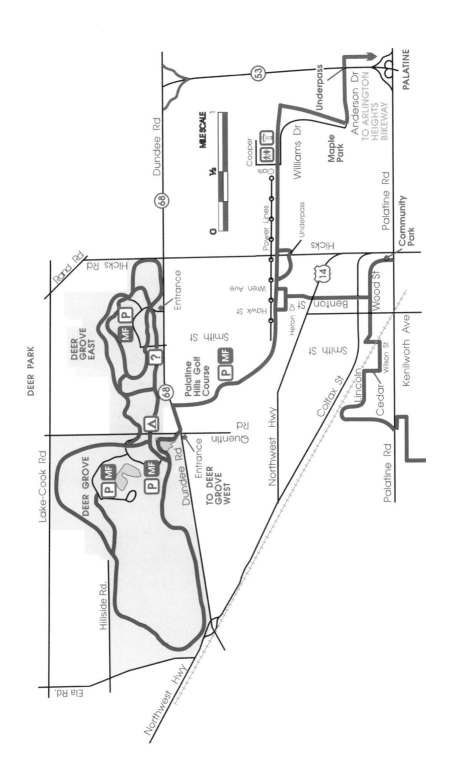

Des Plaines Division

Trail Length   10 miles

Surface   Natural, groomed (5 to 10 feet wide)

Contact   Forest Preserve District of Cook County
                  708-366-8420

The Des Plaines Division has some 4,100 acres that envelop the Des Plaines River Valley. The multi-use trail connects with the Indian Boundary Division at Touhy Avenue and continues northward up the river valley and ending at the Dam No. 1 picnic area for a length of 10 miles, although hikers may continue may continue to the Lake-Cook county line, 2 miles further. The Des Plaines Division offers some of the best area for mountain biking in metropolitan Chicago, and its almost impossible to get lost because it's a linear trail and there are cross streets.

The route measures 5 to 10 feet wide with shade trees bordering on each side. The singletrack trails tend to be close to the river's edge, and may be under water during the rainy season. The terrain is generally flat with only gradual elevation changes. There are several east-west streets to cross. There also is a trail gap between Northwest Highway and Rand Road. Take the Des Plaines River Road for a half mile, north or south, and then east to pick up the trail again.

Wildflowers are abundant and in great variety in the Camp Pine and Lake Avenue Woods Area. White Trillium and other spring wildflowers can be found north of Palatine Road. So take your time on this excursion. Get acquainted with the trees, shrubs, and wildflowers, and watch for wild creatures.

- Low dam with ramp for canoes and rowboats.

- Hard maples with gorgeous fall colors.

- Site of Indian Village.

- Indian Trail Tree.

- Dam No. 2 with large weeping willow on the riverbanks.

- Site of a Pioneer Cabin with hug cottonwoods nearby.

- Indian Portage to North Branch of the Chicago River.

- Dam No. 1

- Indian Charcoal pits and chipping station

- River Trail Nature Center

Getting There   The trail can be accessed from most of the cross streets as illustrated on the map. There are several parking areas providing convenient access from the east side of the river.

Des Plaines Division (continued)

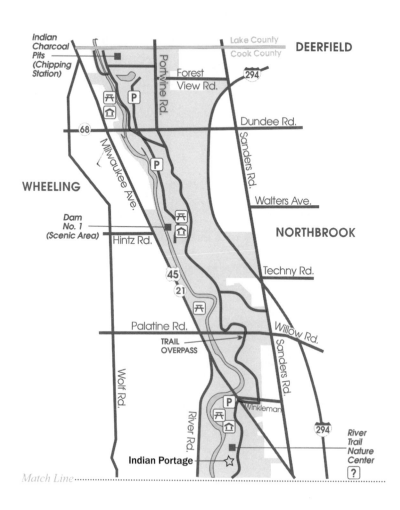

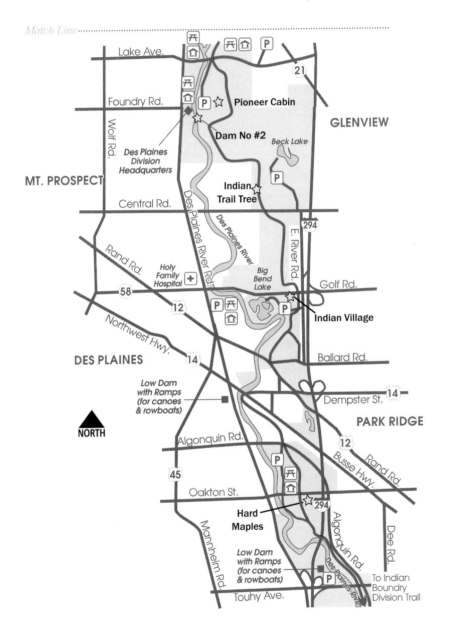

Lake Ave.

21

Foundry Rd.

Pioneer Cabin

GLENVIEW

Wolf Rd.

Des Plaines Division Headquarters

Dam No #2

Beck Lake

MT. PROSPECT

Central Rd.

Des Plaines River Rd.

Des Plaines River

Indian Trail Tree

294

E. River Rd.

Rand Rd.

58

Holy Family Hospital

Big Bend Lake

Golf Rd.

12

Indian Village

Northwest Hwy.

DES PLAINES

14

Ballard Rd.

Low Dam with Ramps (for canoes & rowboats)

Dempster St.

14

NORTH

PARK RIDGE

Algonquin Rd.

12

Busse Hwy.

Rand Rd.

45

Oakton St.

294

Algonquin Rd.

Dee Rd.

Hard Maples

Mannheim Rd.

Low Dam with Ramps (for canoes & rowboats)

Des Plaines River

Touhy Ave.

To Indian Boundry Division Trail

Evanston Bikeways

Trail Length	7 miles
Surface	Asphalt paved
Contact	City of Evanston 847-328-2100

Evanston, home to Northwestern University, is a bicycle-friendly community with tree-lined streets and several parks along Lake Michigan's shores. There are off-road pathways along the lakefront and the North Shore Channel as well as on-road bicycle routes. Bicycle Racks are available throughout the downtown area.

The Lake Shore Pathway is a 5 mile off-road route looping around Northwestern University and following the Lake Michigan shore heading south to Chicago. North of Centennial Park, the bike path runs along Lake Michigan on the east side of the Northwestern University campus. A bridge over a lagoon leads to beautiful views of both the downtown Chicago skyline to the south and the Northwestern campus. The off-road path runs north to Lincoln Street. From there, head west to Sheridan Road. The sidewalk on the east side of Sheridan serves as the bike path north to Ridge Road and south to Centennial Park.

A short distance north of the university you'll come to the Grosse Point Light State and Lighthouse Park. The lighthouse was built in 1873 to remedy the dangerous condition caused by shallow shoals and turbulent wind conditions off the point where many ships had sunk. The visitor/ maritime center is only open on weekends. The lighthouse is also open for tours on weekends. Next-door is the Evanston Art Center, which exhibits contemporary art. A 2 mile on-road bike route beginning at Sheridan Road and Lincoln Street will take you to the Green Bay Trail in Wilmette. To get there head west on Lincoln, north on Asbury Avenue, west of Isabella Street, north on Poplar Avenue, and west on Forest Avenue to Shorewood Park in Wilmette.

Parallel bicycle and pedestrian pathways run south along Lake Michigan for 1 mile from the Northwestern campus through Centennial Park and several others to Greenleaf Street. A sidewalk along the east side of Sheridan Road runs between Calvary Cemetery and Lake Michigan. Water fountains, picnic tables, and restrooms are available in Centennial Park. Some 3.5 miles south of Evanston's city limits is the northern trailhead of the 20 mile Chicago Lakefront Bike Path. Follow the designated bike route signs along the way through the Rogers Park area.

The North Shore Channel connects to Lake Michigan at Wilmette Harbor north of Evanston. From there it runs south 7.5 miles to a merger with the North Branch of the Chicago River south of Foster Avenue in Chicago. There is a 3 mile asphalt trail running east of the Channel through Evanston and Skokie. There is also a multi-use trail running along the west bank of the North Shore Channel for .8 mile south to Oakton and 2 miles north to Green Bay Road. There are a series of overlapping loops of the pathway passing several contemporary sculptures along the way. Farther north in Evanston, you'll find the Ladd Arboretum and the Ecology Center. Here the trail narrows and has a crushed limestone surface. Along this trail is a friendship garden, bird sanctuary, prairie demonstration area, and a windmill demonstrating alternative energy sources. There is also over 2 miles of asphalt path along the east side of the North Shore Channel running through an urban residential area of Evanston.

Evanston Bikeways (continued)

Getting There Take Church Street east through downtown Evanston to Sheridan Road near Lake Michigan. Park south of the university along Sheridan Road. There is a 3-hour free parking limit along Centennial Park. If you're planning on more time, park farther south at Clark Square Park at Kedzie Street and Sheridan.

North Shore Channel Take Main Street in Skokie east of Route 41 to McCormick Boulevard. Head north on McCormick and turn right into the Skokie North Shore Sculpture Park parking area.

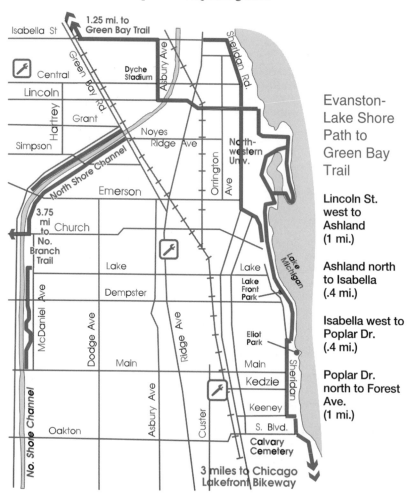

Evanston-
Lake Shore
Path to
Green Bay
Trail

Lincoln St.
west to
Ashland
(1 mi.)

Ashland north
to Isabella
(.4 mi.)

Isabella west to
Poplar Dr.
(.4 mi.)

Poplar Dr.
north to Forest
Ave.
(1 mi.)

Green Bay Trail

Trail Length	6 miles
Surface	Paved
Contact	Winnetka Park District 847-501-2040

The Green Bay Trail runs from Wilmette to the Lake County line. It mostly parallels the Northwestern rail line. In addition to Wilmette, the trail takes you through the picturesque communities of Kenilworth, Winnetka, and Glencoe. This mainly urban to suburban setting provides ample opportunities to enjoy the many eating establishments and beautiful homes along the trail.

If you are starting your ride in Wilmette, park in the designated areas along Green Bay Road or Lake Street one block south. During weekdays, there is a two-hour parking limit. There is also restricted parking near the train station in Kenilworth at Kenilworth Avenue, and Glencoe, north of Park Avenue. Farther north you can park in Turnbull Woods Forest Preserve just south of Lake Cook Road on Green Bay Road, 0.2 miles from the trail.

The surface is asphalt for the first few miles with a few street crossings. The path is mostly a dedicated off-road trail except for the interludes at each community's train station where you'll need to use the street or parking lot. The dedicated trail begins again at the far end of each train station's parking area. In Kenilworth near the train station, watch for the bike route signs. North of the station, the trail proceeds through a park

Green Bay Trail (continued)

and then a few blocks on the street. The off-road path begins again at Ivy Court with a sharp curve going up a small incline.

The next 3 mile stretch is free of road crossings due to a series of road bridges over both the Metra tracks and the Green Bay Trail. Just south of the Hubbard Woods train station is an unmarked underpass at Tower Road. For a brief side trip, note the asphalt path climbing up the embankment to the right of the trail. Take the path up the hill and head right to Tower Road where you will find Winnetka's Tower Road Park 0.3 miles east along Lake Michigan. Here you can walk down the long winding stairs to the beach, or pause at the water fountain for a drink.

In Glencoe, the trail is on-road near the train station. Here Green Bay Road is a lightly used side street through the train station parking area with Glencoe Road serving as the main auto traffic route to the west of the trail. North of downtown Glencoe, the path runs through a shady tunnel of trees with Lake Shore County Club to the east. This is a quiet, peaceful portion of the trail with only faint road sounds. At Lake Cook Road the Green Bay Trail officially ends, but it continues as the Robert McClory Bike Path through Lake County.

Getting There   The southern trailhead is in Shorewood Park at Forest Avenue in Downtown Wilmette, one block east of Green Bay Road.

bluebird

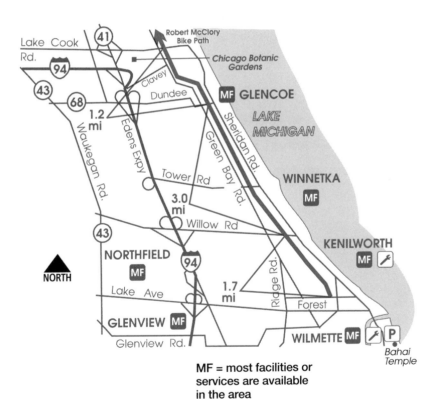

MF = most facilities or
services are available
in the area

Illinois Prairie Path

Trail Length	Illinois Prairie Path	44.2 miles
	Batavia Spur	5 miles
	Geneva Spur	5 miles
	Great Western Trail	11.5 miles
Surface	Limestone screenings (Batavia Spur is partially paved)	
Contact	The Illinois Prairie Path	630-665-5310

The Illinois Prairie Path is a 54.2 mile long trail in Cook, DuPage and Kane Counties (65.7 miles if the DuPage County Great Western Trail is included as a spur). It is open to biking, hiking, jogging, equestrian, and nature trail use. The trail follows the right-of-way of the Chicago, Aurora and Elgin Railway, an electric line that carried commuters and freight between Chicago and the western suburbs as far as communities along the Fox River from Elgin to Aurora starting in 1902. Commuter operations were suspended in 1957 and freight operations in 1959. The right-of-way was finally abandoned in 1961.

In September of 1963, in a letter to the Chicago Tribune, Mrs. May Theilgaard Watts, a distinguished naturalist, teacher and author, outlined a proposal to convert the abandoned right-of-way into a trail through the western suburbs of Chicago. The letter inspired a dedicated group of trail advocates who decided to make the idea a reality. In 1965, Mrs. Watts' group formally established the Illinois Prairie Path (IPP corporation), an Illinois not-for-profit corporation. In 1971, a major portion of the Illinois Prairie Path was designated a National Recreation Trail. The trail was the first in

Illinois to receive this honor. In December, 1979, the Illinois Department of Conservation extended the Illinois Prairie Path's eastern terminus into Cook County by acquiring an additional 4.5 miles of right-of-way.

The Illinois Prairie Path is now managed by various county government agencies due to liability issues, but volunteers through the IPP Corporation are still active in making improvements. These volunteers have built three steel bridges, surfaced miles of trail, installed benches, signs and steps, and preserved prairie remnants, making the Illinois Prairie Path one of the most utilized urban trail in the United States.

In Cook and DuPage County, the trail is 10 foot wide crushed limestone. In Kane County, you will find asphalt as well as crushed limestone segments. There are many street crossings along the path, some in quiet residential areas, and others in busy downtown areas. At most crossings, you'll find a metal post in the center of the trail as well as two posts near the sides of the path to keep out motorized vehicles. If you are biking, take your time and enjoy the parks, forest preserves, communities and other points of interest along the way.

The main stem of the Path has its eastern terminus at First Avenue in Maywood and runs 15 miles west to Wheaton, where it sends one spur 14 miles northwest to connect with the Fox River Trail to Elgin, and a second spur southwest 13 mile to Aurora where you can pick up the Fox River and Virgil Gilman Trails. A spur off the Elgin Spur goes 11 miles west to Geneva, and a spur off the Aurora Spur goes 6 miles west to Batavia. In addition, the Path's main stem connects with the Great

Illinois Prairie Path (continued)

Western Trail in Villa Park (near Villa Street) and runs almost 12 miles west to the Prairie Path's Elgin Spur, ending at Prince Crossing Road in West Chicago. As a result, hikers and bikers have access to the most extensive interconnected trail system in the Chicago area. Since the Illinois Prairie Path connects to the Fox River Trail, which connects to the McHenry County Prairie Trail, you could bike over 100 miles from Maywood to the Wisconsin border on bike trails.

From the trailhead in Maywood, head west on the bridge over Wolf Road to the community of Berkeley. There you will find a park with picnic tables, drinking water, restrooms, and a bike rack west of the bridge. The trail runs under I-294 entering DuPage County at Elmhurst. In Elmhurst, the park district has restored several acres of tallgrass prairies from Salt Creek to Spring Road along the path. At the Berkley Street intersection, there is an interpretive garden labeling native prairie plants. Farther west are bridge crossings at Salt Creek and Route 83. In Villa Park, you will pass the Villa Park Historical Society Museum and Illinois Prairie Path

eastern chipmunk

Visitors Center at Villa Avenue. Continuing on, you enter Lombard where mature trees along the trail provide welcome shade. After passing Lombard, you will pass a large bridge over I-355 as well as a second bridge over the East Branch at the DuPage River. In downtown Glen Ellyn is Prairie Path Park with benches, a water fountain, and a bike rack. The trail continues west into downtown Wheaton to the trailhead at Volunteer Park.

Elgin Branch   From the Wheaton trailhead at Liberty Drive and Carlton Avenue, take the pathway heading north over Volunteer Bridge. In 1983, volunteers restored the 160 foot long iron truss bridge and added three 70 foot spans to cross over two city streets, a small park, and the railroad tracks. This trail segment runs some 16 miles to Elgin where it connects with the Fox River Trail. Past the bridge is the Lincoln Marsh Natural Area. There is an observation platform to your left. A short distance farther northwest is a wooden boardwalk leading to a woodchip nature trail through the marsh, and is limited to hikers. At the County Farm & Geneva Road intersection, the trail slips in two. The Geneva Spur heads west along the south side of Geneva. The Elgin Branch continues in the northwest quadrant of the intersection.

The path continues through marshes along the border of Pratt's Wayne Woods, then crosses over Norton Creek before entering the Preserve. The trail leads first through forest, then wetlands. Leaving the forest preserve, the trail enters Kane County at Dunham Road. Further into Kane County, the woods give way to farmland. It intersects with the Fox River Trail south of Elgin. The Illinois Prairie Path and the Fox River Trail coexist on the same pathway consisting of both off-road and on-street routes

Illinois Prairie Path (continued)

heading north to Prairie Street in Elgin. Follow the bike path signs through Elgin if you want to continue north on the Fox River Trail.

Geneva Spur   This spur runs through Winfield Mounds Forest Preserve, with a bridge crossing over the West Branch of the DuPage River. Past Reed-Keppler Park, the trail crosses on a bridge over several railroad tracks through mostly open prairie and marshland. Farther west you pass the DuPage County Airport to the north and the Prairie Landing public golf course to the south. At East Side Drive, the trail runs north on a sidewalk to High Street. Head west on High Street for a short distance. The off-road path resumes to the right and enters Good Templar Park, crosses over a steep ravine on a bridge and proceeds to a ramp down to Route 25. Across the road, the Spur meets the Fox River Trail.

Aurora Branch   From the northern trailhead at Volunteer Park in

The Illinois Prairie Path

Wheaton, take the limestone path along Carlton Avenue to Roosevelt Road. The off-road trail begins south of Roosevelt Road. There is a crossing at Orchard Road, and again at Wiesbrook Road. Continuing southwest from Wiesbrook Road, the trail is tree-lined and peaceful. Past a tunnel crossing under Butterfield Road the countryside is mostly farmland. Cross Winfield Road at a stoplight, head south along the road for about 300 feet and then west through Warrenville Grove Forest Preserve. As you enter Warrenville, the sidewalk on the west side of Batavia Road is the beginning of the bike path which goes north into Fermilab. There is a single lane tunnel under Route 59, and an underpass at I-88. Past the railroad tracks, and a couple of road crossings you enter the outskirts of Aurora. Cross Route 25 and continue across the road and down a hill into a community park and the southwestern trailhead. The Illinois Prairie Path and the Fox River Trail are contiguous from Illinois Avenue to New York Street where you will find a riverwalk.

Batavia Spur   From practically no trees, the pathway is again tree lined about two miles into the spur. Just west of Fermilab in Kane County is the Kirk Road overpass. West of Fermilab, the trail is asphalt. After crossing Raddant and Hart Road, you will come to the intersection with the Fox River Trail. A mile farther south on the Fox River Trail is the Red Oak Nature Center. The Batavia Spur continues north for a mile contiguous with the Fox River Trail. The west trailhead is at the foot of the stairs leading up to Wilson Street in downtown Batavia.

Getting There   There are many accesses to the Illinois Prairie Path, its branches and spurs.

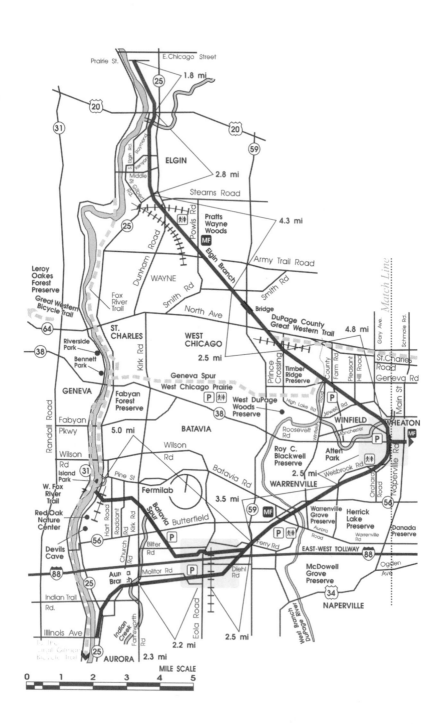

ELGIN BRANCH

ROUTE SLIP	SEGMENT	TOTAL
HWY 38 (Wheaton)		
Jewel Rd. (Wheaton)	1.2	1.2
Prince Crossing	3.6	4.8
Smith Road	2.5	7.3
HWY 25 (S. Elgin)	4.3	11.6
HWY 20 (Elgin)	2.8	14.4
Prairie St. (Elgin)	1.8	16.2

THE ILLINOIS PRAIRIE PATH MAIN STEM

ROUTE SLIP	SEGMENT	TOTAL
HWY 38 (Wheaton)		
Main St. (Glen Ellyn)	2.7	2.7
Du Page River (E. Branch)	1.6	4.3
Westmore Ave. (Lombard)	2.2	6.5
Salt Creek	2.0	8.5
HWY 290 (Elmhurst)	1.8	10.3
Addison Creek	2.7	13.0
First Ave. (Maywood)	2.0	15.0

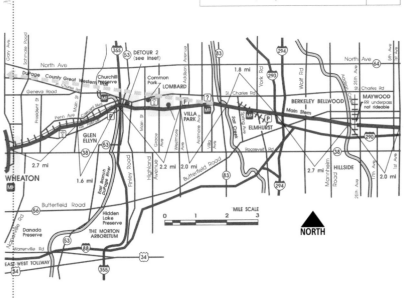

AURORA BRANCH

ROUTE SLIP	SEGMENT	TOTAL
HWY 38 (Wheaton)		
Weisbrook Road	2.5	2.5
Ferry Rd. & HWY 59	3.5	6.0
Eola Rd.	2.5	8.5
Farnsworth Rd. (Aurora)	2.2	10.7
Illinois Ave. (Aurora)	2.3	13.0

Indian Boundary Division

Trail Length	10.8 miles
Surface	Natural, groomed
Contact	Forest Preserve District of Cook County 708-366-9420

Located along the east bank of the Des Plaines River in northwest Cook County. The trail begins at Madison Street, east of First Avenue in Maywood, and follows the Des Plaines River north to Touhy Avenue, east of the Tri-State Tollway in Des Plaines. The trail connects to the Salt Creek Forest Preserve to the south and to the Des Plaines River Division to the north. Expect exposed roots and natural obstructions. Low areas are subject to flooding during the rainy season.

The area is noted for its wildflowers and other vegetation. A great variety of spring wildflowers, huge elms, cottonwoods and silver maples are found in Thatcher Woods. South of Che-Che-Pin-Qual Woods and Schiller Woods skunk cabbage and marsh marigold are found in wet places. White trillium in the spring, blue beech and large sugar maple are common north of Camp Fort Dearborn and Dam No. 4.

Getting There	**Southern trailhead** – The best trail access from a parking area is off Chicago Avenue near the Trailside Museum. **Northern trailhead** – There is parking off Touhy Avenue east of I-294 and west of Talcott Road, or off Devon east of the Des Plaines River.

Points of interest along the Indian Boundary Division include:

- Trailside Museum – exhibits of native animals
- Triton Botanic Garden – summer floral display garden; parking at college
- Evans Field – site of a Indian Village and chipping station. There were several Indian burial places and temporary villages along their main trail following the Des Plaines River. Just east of Evans Field, there are five mounds built by prehistoric Indians.
- Indian Boundary Line – north line of a strip 20 miles wide from Lake Michigan to Ottawa ceded to the whites by the Potawatomi in 1816.
- Part of La Framboise Reserve – granted to a half-breed Indian for aid to the whites at the Fort Dearborn massacre.
- St. Joseph Cemetery – site of Indian Village,
- Model airplane flying field.
- Robinson Reserve – granted to Alexander Robinson (Chief Che-Che-Pin-Qua) for many years of aid to the whites.
- Indian Cemetery – graves of Chief Robinson and family.
- Low dam with ramp for canoes and rowboats.
- "Fountain of Youth" – Water from these wells is believed to be of exceptional quality.

fox

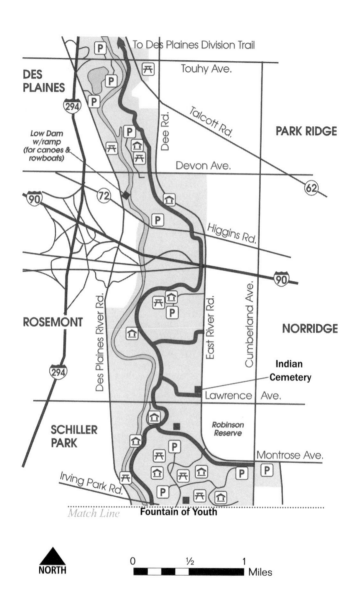

To Des Plaines Division Trail

DES PLAINES

294

Low Dam
w/ramp
(for canoes &
rowboats)

Touhy Ave.

Talcott Rd.

Dee Rd.

PARK RIDGE

Devon Ave.

62

72

90

Higgins Rd.

90

ROSEMONT

Des Plaines River Rd.

East River Rd.

Cumberland Ave.

NORRIDGE

294

Indian
Cemetery

Lawrence Ave.

SCHILLER
PARK

Robinson
Reserve

Montrose Ave.

Irving Park Rd.

Match Line Fountain of Youth

NORTH

0   ½   1
                    Miles

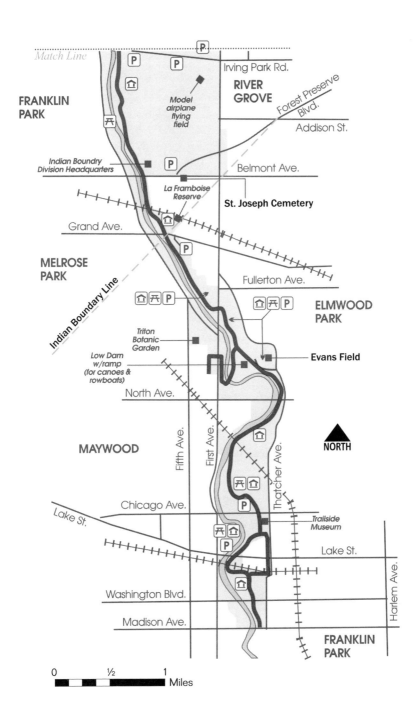

Match Line

FRANKLIN
PARK

RIVER
GROVE

Irving Park Rd.

Forest Preserve Blvd.

Addison St.

Model
airplane
flying
field

Indian Boundry
Division Headquarters

Belmont Ave.

La Framboise
Reserve

St. Joseph Cemetery

Grand Ave.

MELROSE
PARK

Fullerton Ave.

ELMWOOD
PARK

Indian Boundary Line

Triton
Botanic
Garden

Evans Field

Low Dam
w/ramp
(for canoes &
rowboats)

North Ave.

MAYWOOD

Fifth Ave.

First Ave.

Thatcher Ave.

NORTH

Chicago Ave.

Trailside
Museum

Lake St.

Lake St.

Harlem Ave.

Washington Blvd.

Madison Ave.

FRANKLIN
PARK

0   ½   1
Miles

71

John Humphrey Bike Trail

Trail Length	8 miles
Surface	Paved (includes public sidewalks)
Contact	Village of Orland Park, Dept. of Parks 708-403-7275

Over 8 miles of trails and designated sidewalks connect the Orland Park Village Center, the Humphrey Sport Complex, Centennial Park and the 153rd Street Metro Station. While here enjoy the beauty of mature oak trees in John Humphrey Woods and the serenity of the wetlands located west of Ravinia Avenue. Tinley Creek Trail is accessible at the parking lot located at 151st Street and Catalina Drive. When completed the path will be some 20 miles in length.

Getting There

Orland Park is located in southwest Cook County just east of the Will County line. Bicycle racks are available at the 143rd Street and 153rd Street Metro Station, and at Centennial Park.

oregon white oak

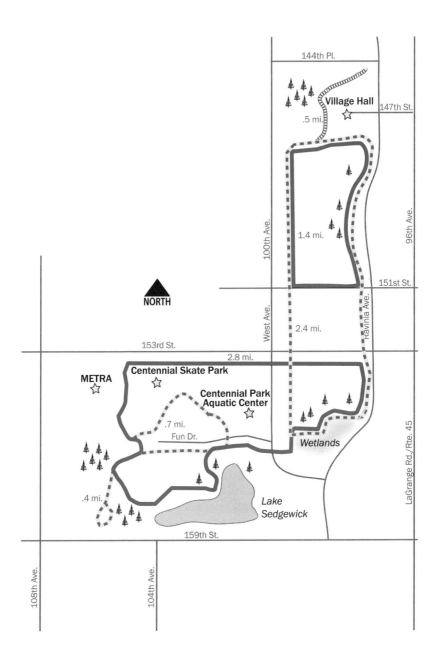

144th Pl.

Village Hall

147th St.

.5 mi.

100th Ave.

96th Ave.

1.4 mi.

NORTH

151st St.

West Ave.

Ravinia Ave.

2.4 mi.

153rd St.

2.8 mi.

METRA

Centennial Skate Park

Centennial Park
Aquatic Center

.7 mi.

Fun Dr.

Wetlands

LaGrange Rd./Rte. 45

.4 mi.

Lake
Sedgewick

159th St.

108th Ave.

104th Ave.

Lake Katherine Nature Preserve

🚶

Trail Length	3.5 miles
Surface	Woodchips, mowed turf
Contact	Lake Katherine Nature Preserve 708-361-1873

Located in community of Palos Heights, this area along the Calumet-Sag
Channel has been converted into a 158 acre nature preserve with a large
lake, prairies, wetlands, a waterfall garden, and a Environmental Learning
Center. Preserve visitors first encounter a picturesque waterfall and small
rippling brook. Ducks swim in the pool at the bottom of the falls. Small
conifers as well as flower and butterfly gardens are located nearby. In
summer you may see hundreds of butterflies sipping nectar from annual
and perennial flowers that have been planted there to attract them.

A walk on the 1 mile woodchip trail surrounding the 20 acre Lake
Katherine leads to an overlook of the Calumet-Sag Channel and plantings
of spruce, pine, and deciduous trees. At the western end of the lake is a
short .5 mile trail through lowlands and a Children's Forest. On the east
side of the lake is a nature center with displays, as well as a children's
theater. Educational programs are offered year round. East of the center
is the Buzz N' Bloom Prairie containing many native prairie species.
A trail through the prairie leads to a footbridge over a bubbling brook
heading east to Harlem Avenue. There is an underpass at Harlem leading
to the 33 acre Eastern Preserve with 2 miles of hiking trails through
woods and prairie. After crossing under Harlem, you will encounter

a massive waterfall flowing into the Cal-Sag Channel. The 2 miles of trail in the Eastern Preserve includes a 1 mile woodchip path paralleling the channel called the Old Canoe Path Trail. A 1 mile Overlook Trail serves to complete a loop back to the nature center. This trail is rugged in spots with tree roots and loose rocks, and sometimes overgrown with vegetation.

Getting There   Located south of the Calumet-Sag Channel. You can take Route 83 east of Route 45 to 75th Avenue. The entrance is at the intersection of Route 83/College Drive and 75th Avenue/Lake Katherine Drive. If traveling by bike or foot you can take the asphalt-paved Tinley Creek Bicycle Trail north from 131st Street for 2 miles to the preserve.

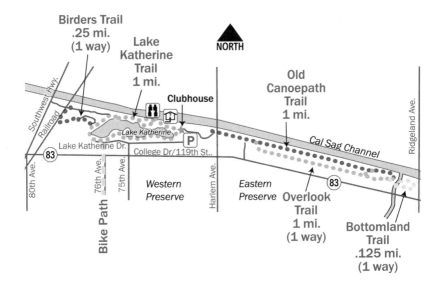

Lemont's I&M Canal Walk & Heritage Quarries Recreation Area

Trail Length	6.8 miles
Surface	Crushed limestone
Contact	Lemont Village Hall 630-257-1550
County	Cook

These trails run along the scenic banks of the I&M Canal. The trails feature spectacular natural views of the Canal and the Des Plaines Valley. They also serve as a link between Heritage Quarries Recreation Area and Lemont's Historic Downtown at General Fry's Landing. The Heritage Quarries Recreation Area adds an additional 3.8 mile trail extension to the existing 3 miles of trails along the original I&M Canal towpath. The trail extension weaves the Heritage Quarries into the original trail. Four pedestrian bridges provide access for hiking and biking in the nearly 300 acre natural area. .

General Fry's Landing, named for the first canal boat to past through Lemont on the I&M Canal in 1848, is located in the heart of Lemont's downtown historic district. The Landing, a park and the I&M Canal interpretive center anchors the recreational trails to Lemont's downtown.

Lemont's Canal walk is a 3.5 miles linear multi-use path running along the I&M Canal in downtown Lemont south of the Chicago Sanitary and Ship Canal. At General Fry's Landing, a small park, you will find benches and a small Friendship Garden.

There are no restrooms or water fountains along the path, but several restaurants are located nearby. The walk is parallel but not part of the Centennial Trail.

Getting There
Take Lemont Road south of I-55 into downtown Lemont. Head east on Illinois Street to Stephen Street. Turn left (north) for three blocks after crossing the I&M Canal to the trail access. Trail parking is available along the canal near the Water Reclamation Plant.

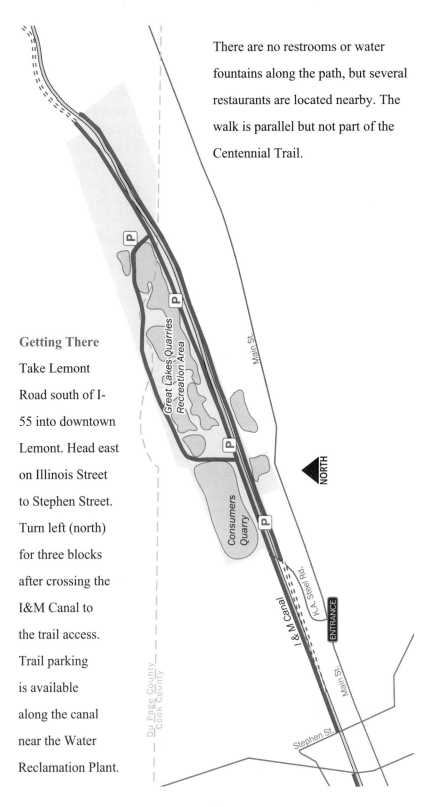

North Branch Bicycle Trail

[bicycle] [hiking] [cross-country skiing]

Trail Length	20 miles
Surface	Asphalt
Contact	Forest Preserve District of Cook County
	708-366-9420

The North Branch Bicycle Trail is a 20 mile paved asphalt bicycle trails running along the Skokie Lagoons and the North Branch of the Chicago River from the Botanic Garden at Lake Cook Road in Glencoe to Caldwell and Devon Avenue on the north side of Chicago. The general setting is open spaces and woods. This is a very popular trail with bicyclists, hikers, runners, and rollerbladers and can get busy, especially on weekends.

Some 10,000 years ago, Lake Chicago, fed by melting glaciers, covered the North Shore. As the water level receded, a large marsh area was formed. The Skokie River, the Middle Fork, and the West Fork flowed south through the marsh to create the North Branch of the Chicago River. The Pottawattamie called the marsh Chewab Skokie or "big wet prairie". This wetland was filled with wildflowers, tall grasses and wildlife. In the 1920's, the fertile soil attracted developers who drained the marsh to use the land for growing crops. However, they did not understand the nature of the wetlands. In spring, the entire area would flood including nearby roads and residential areas. In the fall, dry peat beds would catch on fire and burn for weeks.

By the 1930's, the Forest Preserve District acquired most of the land along the Skokie River. The Civilian Conservation Corps (CCC) formed during the Depression, was charged with building a series of lagoons to stop the flooding. Dams and dikes were used to maintain the water level. The seven Skokie lagoons situated between Dundee and Willow Roads became popular recreation areas. Over the years soil erosion resulting from extensive residential and business construction filled in a significant portion of the lagoons. Beginning in the late 1980's, extensive dredging operations have restored the lagoons. Native grasses and wildflowers have been planted along the Skokie River in the Botanic Garden to help restore the wetlands.

The ride being described for you now starts at the Botanic Garden main entrance and heads south. Biking on the pathways and trails at the Botanic Garden is not allowed. There is a large bike rack area near the Visitor's Center south of parking are #1. To access the bike path, follow the auto road west past the parking areas to a service road heading south. This spot provides one of the most gorgeous views in Chicagoland. To your right across the lake is the Waterfall and Japanese Gardens. There are benches nearby if you want to pause to take in the beautiful scenery.

The 1.2 mile service road leads to a crossing at Dundee Road where the bike path exits the Botanic Garden. Along the way you will pass by several gardens, including Evening Island. There is a pedestrian button at the Dundee Road crossing. South of Dundee a trail intersection offers paths heading both east and west of the Skokie Lagoons. The path to the right leads south along I-94 with more woodland but heavy traffic sounds. The asphalt trail is well maintained with a gently rolling terrain. The next street crossing is at Tower Road a little over 3 miles out, assuming you took the shorter western route along I-94. Here the two pathways merge into a single trail heading south.

Along the way, you'll pass by a boat launch area. The Skokie Lagoons area has become a popular waterway for canoeists. You will also notice a split rail fence separating the asphalt bike path from a paralleling gravel trail. This is a multi-use trail used by equestrians, hikers, and occasionally, mountain bikers.

The next road crossing is Willow Road at Lagoon Drive, 4.7 miles out. Here the lagoons end and flow back into the Skokie River as it heads south. The bike trail separates from the river running farther west. After a crossing at Winnetka Road and the underpass of busy I-94, you'll come to another trail intersection. Stay to the left to keep on the main trail. There is a map on a signpost at the intersection. The 0.4 mile side trail leads back up to Winnetka Road. Nearby the Skokie River and the Middle Fork merge into the North Branch of the Chicago River.

Following the overpass on Lake Street (7 miles out), the terrain becomes hilly and curvy. South of Lake Street, you'll pass a series of forest preserve picnic areas, where you will find restrooms, water pumps, picnic tables, and shelters. The trail parallels Harms Road for some distance. After road crossings at Glenview and Golf Road, you'll pass the Northwestern Equestrian Center just south of Golf Road. Some distance west of the trail in Morton Grove the West Fork joins up to complete the North Branch of the Chicago River.

Following crossings at Beckwith Road and Dempster at 11.2 miles out, you'll pass through the Miami Woods Prairie restoration site. South of here the trail runs through woods on a small bluff overlooking the river to the east. Following another overpass at Oakton Street, the terrain becomes even more hilly and large oak trees line the trail. There are road crossings at Howard Street and Touhy Avenue. At Touhy take the sidewalk east to the light and use the pedestrian button. After the last crossing at Harts Road, you'll come first to the Bunker Hill and then to the Caldwell Woods Preserve picnic areas. The path to the right leads over a creek to the toboggan slide and on to Devon Avenue (15.2 miles out). The trail to the left runs another 1.2 miles east to the southern trailhead at Devon and Caldwell Avenue.

In addition to the bike path just described there is an 8 mile multi-use trail that runs along the river from Tower Road in Winnetka to Dempster Street in Morton Grove. This trail is open to hikers, equestrians, and bicyclists. The trail surface is a combination of earth, cinders, and crushed limestone. It parallels the bike path for much of the route. Washouts and exposed roots are common near the river, and it's easy to get lost so bring a compass if you choose to use this trail.

Getting There To access the northern trailhead, take Lake Cook Road to the Chicago Botanic Garden east of I-94/41 and 0.5 mile west of Greenbay Road. You can also take Lake Cook Road west on the sidewalk on the north side of Lake Cook Road.

To access the southern trailhead, take Milwaukee Avenue to Devon Avenue. Head 0.2 mile east to the Caldwell Woods Preserve. Take the entrance road identified as "Caldwell Woods Groves 1,2, & 3". There are also many forest preserve accesses along the way with available parking. These include Tower Road east of I-94, Willow Road east of I-94, Lake Avenue west of I-94, Harms Road, south of Glenview Road, Harts Road east of Milwaukee Avenue, and Caldwell Avenue south of Touhy Avenue.

POINTS OF INTEREST	
(A)	Chicago Botanic Garden
(B)	Skokie Lagoons
(C)	Blue Star Memorial Woods
(D)	Glenview Woods
(E)	Harms Woods
(F)	Chick Evans Golf Course
(G)	Linne Woods
(H)	Miami Woods
(I)	Clayton Smith Woods
(J)	Whealan Pool
(K)	Edgebrook Golf Course
(L)	Billy Caldwell Golf Course

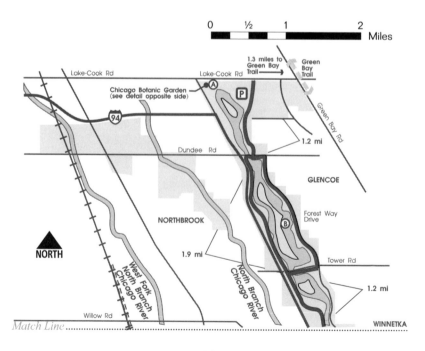

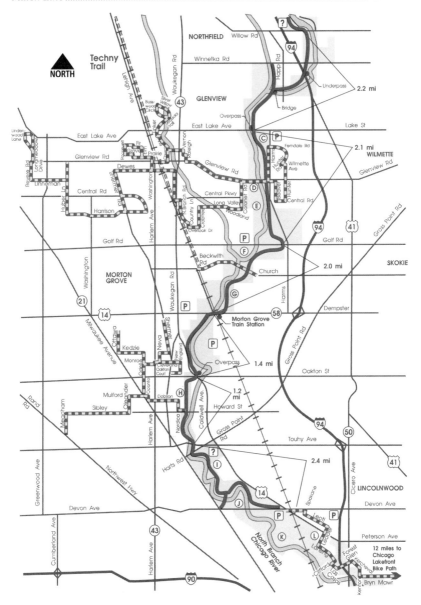

━━━━━━ Alternate Bike Trail

Match Line ....

0   ½   1   2
▰▰▰▰▰▰▰▰▰▰▰ Miles

NORTH

Techny
Trail

NORTHFIELD

Willow Rd

Winnetka Rd

Lehigh Ave

Waukegan Rd

Happ Rd

94

Underpass   2.2 mi

Bridge

GLENVIEW

43

Overpass

East Lake Ave

Lake St

Linden-
wood
Lane

East Lake Ave

East Lake Ave

C   P

Ferndale Rd   2.1 mi

Revere Rd

Longmeadow
Drive

Glenview Rd

Fir
Prairie

WILMETTE

Linneman

Dewes

Glenview Rd

Wilmette
Ave

Glenview Rd

Harms

Harbor Ln

Central Rd

Washington

Central Pkwy

Central Rd

D

Harrison

Long Valley

Woodland

Overlook Dr

E

Colonial Rd

Harlem Ave

Golf Rd

Country Ln

P

F

Golf Rd

94

41

Grass Point Rd

Beckwith
Rd

Church

2.0 mi

SKOKIE

MORTON
GROVE

Waukegan Rd

G

Harms

Dempster

21

14

58

Milwaukee Avenue

Ottawa

P

Morton Grove
Train Station

Grass Point Rd

Kedzie

Neva

New England

Oakton St

Monroe

Cleveland

Overpass   1.4 mi

Cass

Oakton Court

Oconto

1.2
mi

Mulford

Dobson

H

94

50

Oleander

Sibley

Nordica

Caldwell Ave

Howard St

41

Mecham

Harlem Ave

Grass Point
Rd

Touhy Ave

Cicero Ave

Rand
Rd

?

2.4 mi

LINCOLNWOOD

Greenwood Ave

Northwest Hwy

I

Harts Rd

14

Devon Ave

Devon Ave

J

P

P

Cumberland Ave

43

K

L

Peterson Ave

Harlem Ave

North Branch
Chicago River

Scott

12 miles to
Chicago
Lakefront
Bike Path

Forest
Glen

Kentone

90

Lowell

Clifford

Bryn Mawr

Kenton

North Park Village Nature Center

Trail Length	2.5 miles
Surface	Woodchip
Information	North Park Village Nature Center 312-744-5472

A 46 acre facility on Chicago's northside where you can hike through 2.5 miles of forest, wetlands, prairie, and savannah. Between 1911 and 1974 this site served as a sanitarium for tuberculosis patients. There are still some old concrete sidewalks along the 10-foot –wide woodchip trails. A retirement community now fills a portion of the former sanitarium grounds.

The trail loops through old savanna, along a pond, and on a boardwalk over a marsh area. Further west the trail leads to the Bluebird Prairie. The trails are limited to hiking. Tallgrass species such as Indian grass grow to 6 feet or taller in the fall. Interpretive signs can be found to describe the natural heritage of the ecosystems present here. The center provides an animal room with turtles, snakes and salamanders, as is popular with children. Hours are 10 am to 4 pm daily, except Thanksgiving, Christmas, and New Year's Day. There is no admission fee.

Getting There   Take Peterson Avenue east of I-94 to Pulaski Road. Head south for 0.2 miles to North Park Village. Drive past the guard station and go left at the stop sign following the road to the nature center.

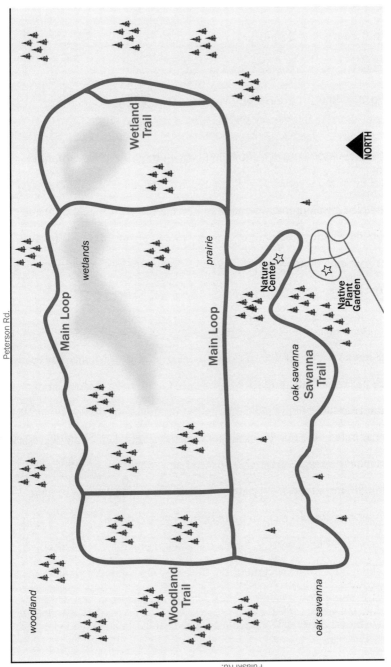

Peterson Rd.

Pulaski Rd.

Wetland Trail

Main Loop

Main Loop

Woodland Trail

Savanna Trail

Nature Center

Native Plant Garden

wetlands

prairie

oak savanna

oak savanna

woodland

NORTH

Old Plank Road Trail

Trail Length	21 miles
Surface	Asphalt, 10 feet wide
Information	Forest Preserve District of Will County 815-727-8700

During the 1800's, early settlers in northern Illinois had the difficult task of moving wagons of grain and household goods on dirt roads that connected rapidly growing communities and farms. With spring thaws and rains, the dirt roads became murky mire. One solution was to cover the dirt road with planks or wood laid side-by-side that provided a drier more stable surface. But by the 1880's the planks roads were largely replaced, sometimes by more efficient railway lines.

In the late 1970's, the Forest Preserve District of Will County and many other agencies, including Rich Township, the Illinois Department of Natural Resources, and the communities of Frankfort, Matteson, and Park Forest, formed the Old Plank Road Management Commission to preserve a 20 mile greenway on the right-of-way of an abandoned Penn Central rail line. The goal was to establish an east-west trail through wetlands, prairies, woodlands, and communities of Cook and Will Counties from Joliet east to Park Forest. After many years of planning and consensus building, a 13.1 mile section of the trail was opened in the summer of 1997, running from Hickory Creek Junction Preserve, in Will County, east to Park Forest, in Cook County. The trail has been extended an

Old Plank Road Trail (continued)

additional 7 miles west to Park Road, in Joliet Township, with the final mile to Washington Street being completed in 2006.

The Old Plank Road Trail is major link in the Grand Illinois Trail. Hickory Creek Junction, a half mile north of the trail, serves as an access point with parking and a pedestrian bridge over Highway 30. A half mile east of the trail's east trailhead is the Sauk Trail Woods and bicycle trail. The setting is urban with open and some wooded area.

Getting There   There are numerous opportunities to park and access

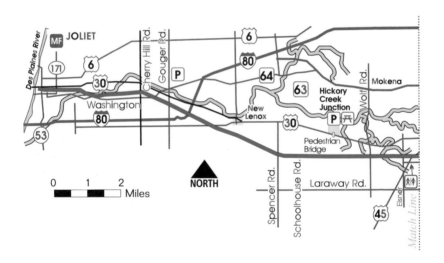

the trail in the communities along the route. There is currently no designated parking at the eastern trailhead at Western Avenue. A good place to park is on the east side at Logan Park in Park Forest west of Orchard Drive and south of Route 30. Another good place to park is in Frankfort. Take Route 45 south of Route 30 to White Street. Proceed south a half mile to Kansas Street. Parking is available to the right next to the village green, which is adjacent to the trail. To get to Hickory Creek Preserve, located in Mokena, take Route 30 (Lincoln Highway) west of Route 45 or east of Schoolhouse Road to the entrance.

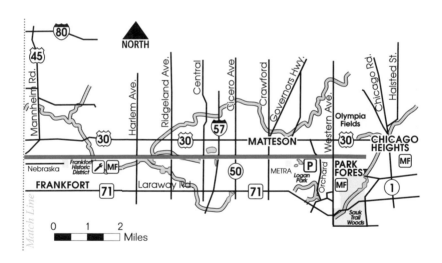

Palatine Trails & Bikeways

Trail Length   15 miles (includes connecting street routes)

Surface   Paved

Contact   Palatine Park District   847-991-0333

Palatine is located in northwest Cook County. It extends throughout the Palatine Park District, combining some 6 miles of paved trail with designated side streets. The trail provides access to schools, Harper College, neighborhood parks, Palatine Hills Golf Course, and other points of interest.

The paved trail in the northern section starts at Maple Park off of Williams. This part of the trail goes through residential areas, and there are a number of residential streets to cross. At Hicks Road there is an underpass, after which you go through a little wooded area around the Palatine Public Library. Past Smith Road you enter an area with woods on one side and a Golf Course on the other, followed by a lake with a pavilion. Just past the lake and after a bridge, you'll be going up a somewhat steep hill. The trail ends at Dundee Road and across from the Deer Grove Forest Preserve.

The paved trail in the southern section begins off Algonquin Road just west of Quentin Road and east of Harper Community College. Past Euclid Avenue, you'll continue through a number of designated side streets as you continue north, eventually arriving at Maple Park.

Getting There   There are numerous accesses. To get to Maple Park, take Palatine Road west of Route 53 to Williams Drive. Maple Park is located a few blocks north on Williams.

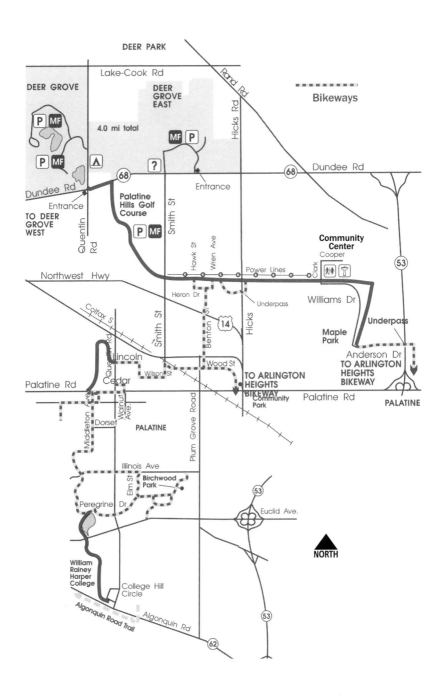

DEER PARK

Lake-Cook Rd

Rand Rd

Hicks Rd

Bikeways

DEER GROVE

DEER GROVE EAST

4.0 mi total

P   MF

P   MF

A

68

Dundee Rd

MF   P

Entrance

68   Dundee Rd

Entrance

TO DEER GROVE WEST

Quentin Rd

?

Palatine Hills Golf Course

P   MF

Smith St

53

Community Center
Cooper

Northwest Hwy

Hawk St

Wren Ave

Power Lines

Clark

Heron Dr

Underpass

Williams Dr

Underpass

Colfax S

Smith St

Benton St

14

Hicks

Maple Park

Anderson Dr
TO ARLINGTON HEIGHTS BIKEWAY

Lincoln

Cedar

Queens Rd

Wilson St

Wood St

TO ARLINGTON HEIGHTS BIKEWAY

Palatine Rd

PALATINE

Palatine Rd

Community Park

Palatine Rd

Walnut Ave.

Middleton Ave.

Dorset

PALATINE

Illinois Ave

Plum Grove Road

Elm St

Birchwood Park

53

Peregrine Dr

Euclid Ave.

NORTH

William Rainey Harper College

College Hill Circle

Algonquin Road Trail   Algonquin Rd

53

62

53

91

Palos & Sag Valley Forest Preserves

Trail Length	32 miles
Surface	Both natural & groomed
Information	Palos Forest Preserve 708-361-1536
County	Cook

Chicagoland's largest county forest preserve site. Palos and Sag Valley together encompass more than 14,000 acres of woods, prairie, and wetland in a hilly triangle with nine mile sides. You'll discover over 32 miles of unpaved, multi-use trails through the Palos Preserves as well as many miles of additional footpaths branching from the main trail. Two deep valleys slice between two high mounds of glacial debris, called moraines. Early settlers called the Palos Moraine in the north "Mount Forest Island", because its forested hills rose 150 feet above the flat prairie that stretched toward Lake Michigan. The trail network enables visitors to hike, bike and ski across miles of natural contours while avoiding most roads. It's a great way to appreciate the pockets of restored native habitat in the environment of a landscape that still needs much restoration attention. There are signposts at each intersection and color-coded wands every quarter mile, making it easier to stay on designated trails.

To get a sense of the glacial scale of these preserves, take a walk on the Ester Trail, a footpath looping up the southern moraine in the Cap Sauers Holdings, an Illinois Nature Preserve. From the top of the trail, the valley stretches out through the treetops to the Palos Moraine a mile away.

Continuing along the esker's ridge, hikers will come to Visitation Prairie. This is as deep in wilderness as it gets in Cook County. Pause and listen to the landscape, silent of traffic, with only the soft rustle grass to break the stillness.

More than a century ago, Palos Hills farmers sent their children to school in a one-room log cabin near what is now the busy intersection of 95th Street and La Grange Road. Classes continued until 1948. In 1952 the Forest Preserve District of Cook County converted the building to a nature center. Inside, visitors of all ages can peer inside tanks with field mice, turtles, and frogs, or observe busy bees perform intricate dances spinning in circles, moving forward and back. These dances give exact directions to where other bees can find flowers producing nectar they need to make their honey. Back outside, the White Oak and Black Oak

Palos & Sag Valley Forest Preserves (continued)

footpaths offer one mile circuits through open woodlands. West of the schoolhouse is the 5.2 mile Palos Yellow Trail. The Yellow Trail head northeast to the high quality restored savanna of Spear Woods, where side-meanders skirt small sloughs and you may spot beaver and muskrat lodges.

The longest loop in the system is the eight mile Sag Valley Yellow Trail. Starting at the Swallow Cliff parking lot, the wide trail hugs the base of the bluff as it heads eastward. It eventually circles southwest to McClaughry Springs, an enchanting spot, especially in winter with its beautiful seeps. The Trail climbs to the top of the moraine above McClaughry, heading a mile west, where you can choose to weave through the Laughing Squaw Sloughs and continue west, or cut the trip short and head to the top of Swallow Cliff for a view across the Sag Valley, named for the former Saganashkee Swamp.

On the far west side of the Palos Preserves south of the Cal-Sag Channel you will find Camp Sagawau, open by reservation only. Here you can hike through Cook County's only natural rock canyon. Special programs include a canyon hike in which participants wade through a creek to enjoy the ferns, wildflowers, and rock formations. In spring, lush green ferns begin to unfold from closed fiddle-like branches to lacy green delights. Naturalists will also lead you on fossil hunts, and in the winter, you can participate in Nordic ski clinics. For more information on how to take a trip through this unique area call 630-257-2045.

At Tampier Lake you'll find another 4.5 miles of unpaved, multi-use trails south of McCarthy Road and west of Wolf Road. The .9 mile section south of Tampier Lake along 135th Street is relatively flat, bumpy, and not very interesting except for a nice view of the lake. The trail crosses Will-Cook Road and heads northwest through a large open field on a service road. North of 131st Street the trail becomes more interesting as it meanders through woods and open meadow before it dead ends at a slough.

Getting There   Due to the enormous size and scope of the Palos Preserves, parking locations are innumerable, but the following are recommended places to park that provide easy trail access to the nature centers and the multi-use trails.

Little Red Schoolhouse - North of the Cal-Sag Channel, from the Willow Springs Road intersection with Archer Avenue south of the Des Plaines River, take Willow Springs south of 95th Street. Here Willow Springs becomes 104th Avenue. Proceed south. The Little Red Schoolhouse Nature Center entrance is on the west side. You can access the multi-use trail south of the parking lot where it intersects with the nature center path leading to the White Oak Trail.

Sag Valley - Take Route 83 south to the Swallow Cliff Toboggan Slide entrance .2 miles west of 96th Avenue (Route 45).

Camp Sagawau - Take Route 83 (111th Street) south of the Cal-Sag Channel and east of Archer Avenue. Proceed east for a short distance to the Camp Sagawau entrance on the north side of Route 83.

Tampier Lake Multi-Use Trail - Take Will-Cook Road south of McCarthy Road and 131st Street to the Tampier Lake entrance .1 mile south of 131st Street on the east side.

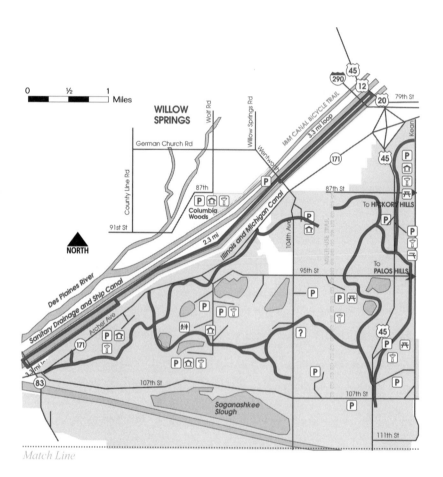

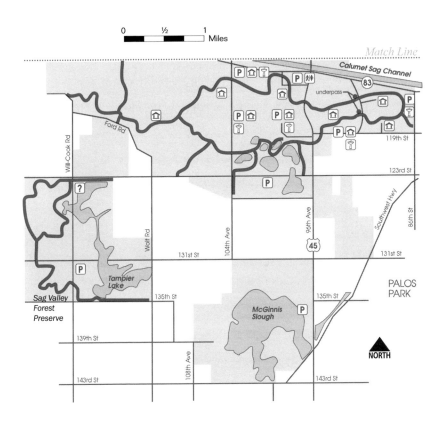

0   ½   1
Miles

Calumet Sag Channel

83

underpass

119th St

123rd St

Ford Rd

Will-Cook Rd

Wolf Rd

104th Ave

96th Ave

Southwest Hwy

86th St

45

131st St

131st St

PALOS PARK

Tampier Lake

131st St

135th St

135th St

McGinnis Slough

Sag Valley Forest Preserve

NORTH

139th St

108th Ave

143rd St

143rd St

97

Poplar Creek Forest Preserve Trail

Trail Length	9.5 miles
Surface	Asphalt
Contact	Forest Preserve District of Cook County 708-366-9420

The 4,500 acre Poplar Creek Forest Preserve is located in the far northwest reaches of Cook County. The paved trail loops around the preserve, passing through scenic forest area and meadows. There are several moderate, lengthy inclines along the route. The preserve is bordered by Hoffman Estates to the east, west and south, and South Barrington to the north. Toilets, water and picnic facilities are located near a number of the parking areas. Portions of the preserve have been restored to original Illinois Prairie.

There are also several miles of dirt, single-track mountain bike/equestrian trail that branch off west of Route 59 on both side of Golf Road (Route 58), traveling the western expanses of the preserve from Schaumburg Road to I-90. This is a more heavily wooded area of the preserve. You can access these dirt trails from the back of the picnic area off Route 59, follow the grass path heading southwest from the Route 58/59 intersection, or by following the gravel path northwest at 59 and Shoe Factory Road and then crossing Show Factory when you come to the railroad tracks.

Getting There The entrance is on the west side of Barrington Road, south of West Higgins Road and the Northwest Tollway (I-90).

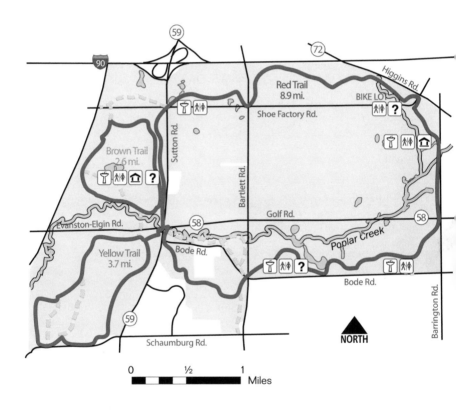

River Trail Nature Center

Trail Length   1.5 mile

Surface   Groomed

Contact   River Trail Nature Center   847-824-8360

The River Trail Nature Center is located in the Des Plaines Division, bordered on the east by the Des Plaines Division Trail and on the west by the Des Plaines River. The trails associated with this nature center consist of three half mile loops: The Green Bay Trail, Little Fort Trail and Grove Partridge Trail.

A couple hundred of years ago American Indians paddled their canoes along the river and hunted bears, deer and elk along its banks, while trappers and fur traders came searching for beaver in its waters. A fragment of that time has been preserved here. River Trail Nature Center tells the story of native plants and animals that remain in the urban environment. Here you can walk through the sugar maple woods along the river, the hallmark of the three miles of self-guiding trails surrounding the Nature Center.

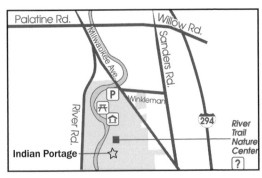

The Visitor Center maintains live animal displays featuring raptors and animals native to the area, beehives producing local wildflower honey. There is also an amphitheater with programs for groups, families and special audiences.

Getting There   From the intersection of Milwaukee Avenue and Winkelman Road, go south on Milwaukee Avenue a little less than a half mile to a entrance road on the right. Parking is available by the Visitor Center.

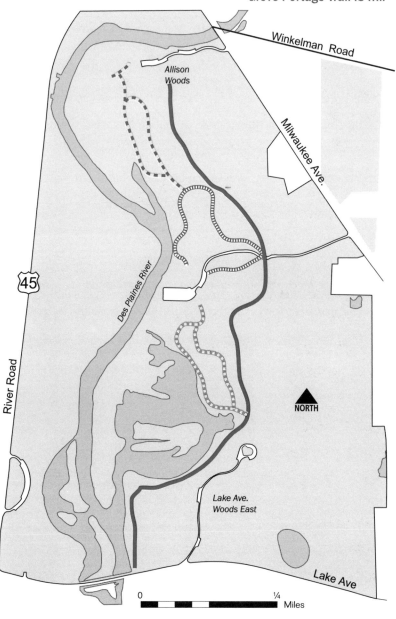

Green Bay Trail .5 mi.
Little Fort Trail .5 mi.
Grove Portage Trail .5 mi.

Winkelman Road

Allison Woods

Milwaukee Ave.

45

Des Plaines River

River Road

NORTH

Lake Ave. Woods East

Lake Ave

0   ¼
          Miles

Salt Creek Greenway

Salt Creek runs through northwestern Cook County, and then flows south to DuPage County before heading back east into central Cook County where it empties into the Des Plaines River south of Brookfield. The Salt Creek has several forest preserves along its shores providing habitat for wildlife. There are also many trails in these forest preserves and communities along the creek.

There is no salt water in the creek today, but there is a story that the name Salt Creek came from a 19th century farmer's mishap. His wagon, loaded with salt barrels, got stuck in the water during a crossing. The next day he discovered the salt had washed into the creek, thus this misadventure continues to live on. By the 1970's, with all the development in the western suburbs, water quality had deteriorated badly. With the introduction of more effective sewage treatment and the establishment of natural area greenway surrounding the creek, water quality is much improved, and waterfowl and other wildlife have returned.

You'll find trails at three sites along the Salt Creek Greenway in central Cook County.

Salt Creek Forest Preserve Trail

🚲 🎿 🚶

Trail Length	6.6 miles
Surface	Asphalt
Contact	Forest Preserve District of Cook County 708-366-9420

Located in west central Cook County. Bordered clockwise by the communities of Oakbrook, Westchester, Brookfield, LaGrange Park, LaGrange, and Hinsdale. The Salt Creek starts in Bemis Woods South and continues east to Brookfield Woods, directly across from the Brookfield Zoo. As the trail follows Salt Creek, it provides access to various picnic groves and other points of interest. The trail is winding and has some hills. There are five road crossings and several forest preserves along the way. A new bridge across Salt Creek offers a scenic view with tree branches overhanging the creek. Narrow side trails head off along the creek and into the woods. Hugging the creek in spots, the trail runs mostly through mature woodlands.

For a side trip to the Brookfield Zoo, head east on 31st Street for .2 miles from the eastern trailhead at Brookfield Woods. The Forest Preserve District of Cook County owns and The Chicago Zoological Society operates this world-famous zoo. Here you can observe more than 2,500 animals of 400 different species and enjoy a relaxing walk. For hours and admission prices call 708-485-0263.

Getting There   The trail may be accessed from Ogden Avenue, just east of Wolf Road, or from 31st Street between 1st Avenue and Prairie Avenue.

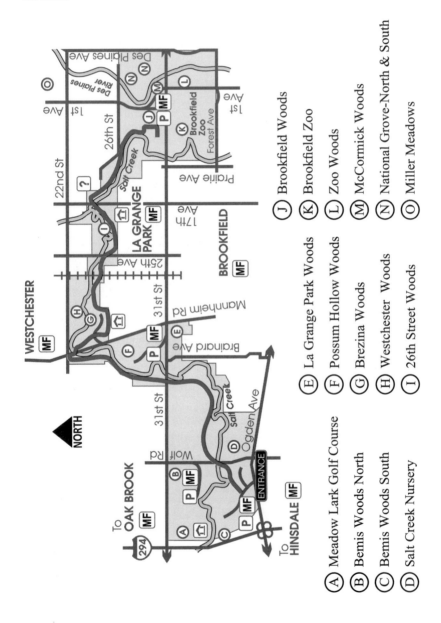

(J) Brookfield Woods
(K) Brookfield Zoo
(L) Zoo Woods
(M) McCormick Woods
(N) National Grove-North & South
(O) Miller Meadows

(E) La Grange Park Woods
(F) Possum Hollow Woods
(G) Brezina Woods
(H) Westchester Woods
(I) 26th Street Woods

(A) Meadow Lark Golf Course
(B) Bemis Woods North
(C) Bemis Woods South
(D) Salt Creek Nursery

Sand Ridge Nature Center

Trail Length	3.8 miles
Surface	Packed dirt, boardwalk
Contact	Sand Ridge Nature Center 708-868-0606

Sand Ridge Nature Center is a 235 acre preserve, with some 3.5 miles of hiking trails. Each trail features different habitats, including prairies, oak savannas, marshes, ponds, woodlands, and ancient sand dunes. Near the cabins, the half mile Redwing Trail circles through oak forests and shrubs. Just north of the Redwing Trail, there is a manmade pond that attracts herons and egrets in the spring and early summer. West of the pond is a 633-foot boardwalk that links with a dirt trail and passes marshy areas. The trail then skirts several prairies where you can observe turtlehead and prairie lily, goldenrod, and sunflowers. After entering woodlands, the trail eventually joins Lost Beach Trail, a 1.5 mile loop around a forested beach ridge and sand dune.

The Nature Center features both the natural history and the cultural history of the Calumet region. Within the building are interpretive displays, as well as native local wildlife. Outside, you can stroll through a colorful butterfly garden, and a vegetable and herb garden displaying plants used by pioneers and Native Americans. There are also several reproduction log cabins on site which depict the lifestyles of early 19th century settlers in this area. Pioneer demonstrations are held most Wednesday mornings from May through November. Special events are held periodically throughout the year. In April there is Earth

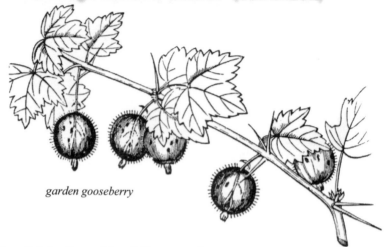

garden gooseberry

Day Celebration, with wildflower walks, special interpretive displays, exhibitors, and more. International Migratory Bird Day is held during May. Illinois Archaeology Day, a celebration of our past, is held in mid-September. On the Sunday before Thanksgiving, Settler's Day is held, featuring costumed re-enactors from our Nation's history, from French fun trading days through the American Revolution and the Civil War. The Christmas Past celebration features a quiet pioneer Christmas from pioneer days.

As the glacier that shaped Lake Michigan receded and lake levels fluctuated, beaches and sand dunes were deposited on a changing shoreline. In time, prairies and woodlands grew on the sandy soils of these ancient shorelines. Today, the Sand Ridge Nature Center stands on a 6,000-year-old broad, low ridge of sand and beach pebbles.

Getting There   Sand Ridge Nature Center is located at 15890 Paxton Avenue in South Holland. From I-94, exit east on 159th Street. Continue on 159th Street past four stoplights to Paxton. Turn left on Paxton. The entrance is located two blocks further on the right.

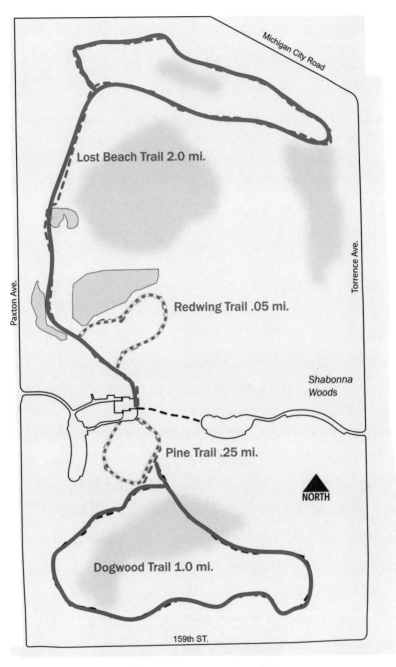

Michigan City Road

Lost Beach Trail 2.0 mi.

Paxton Ave.

Torrence Ave.

Redwing Trail .05 mi.

Shabonna Woods

Pine Trail .25 mi.

NORTH

Dogwood Trail 1.0 mi.

159th ST.

0   600
Feet

Spring Creek Valley Forest Preserve

Trail Length	Undetermined maze
Surface	Mowed turf
Contact	Forest Preserve District of Cook County 708-366-9420

This preserve is probably one of the lesser known and least visited forest preserves in Cook County. The forest preserve, with some 3,900 acres, is comprised of two major, comparably sized plots divided by Dundee Road. Only the southern section provides public parking facilities. The preserve will provide you an opportunity to explore a large, undeveloped, and unmarked landscape. You can easily spend the better part of a day walking the trails south of Dundee Road. A compass or a good sense of direction is a must. You can also visit the northern section of the preserve via a tunnel beneath Dundee Road.

A maze of mowed walking and horse trails criss-crosses the preserve from its southern boundary at Higgins Road north to Dundee Road. The paths meander through the patchwork landscape of woodlands, fields, ponds, and wetlands. Sightings of nesting orchard orioles, yellow-breasted chats, willow flycatchers, and blue-winged warblers are common. To the west, the oak woodlands around Beverly Lake teams with migrating songbirds in mid May. White-tailed deer, red fox and gray fox are often spotted. A good variety of amphibians and reptiles also make their homes in the ponds and fields.

Getting There   **Penny Road Pond parking area** From I-90, exit at Route 59 North. Take Route 59 to Penny Road. Turn left (west) for about a mile to the well-marked entrance on the left.

Dog Training Area and Beverly Lake parking lots From I-90, exit at Route 59 North. Take Route 59 to Higgins Road (Route 72). Turn left (west) and proceed for about a mile to the Dog Training Area, or a bit further to Beverly Lake, both on the north side of Higgins.

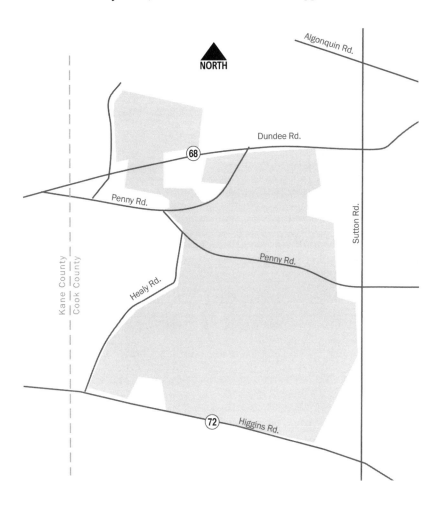

Spring Valley Nature Sanctuary

Trail Length	3 miles
Surface	Groomed
Contact	Schaumburg Park District 847-985-2115

Spring Valley features over 3 miles of handicapped-accessible hiking trails and a museum with natural history displays and information. The Nature Sanctuary is a refuge of 135 acres of fields, forests, marshes and streams. The Vera Meineke Nature Center includes hands-on exhibits, discovery niches and a natural history library. The grounds are open from 8 am to 8 pm April through October and 8 am to 5 pm November through March. The visitor center is open 9 am to 5 pm daily. Nature programs are offered throughout the year.

The 1.2 mile Illinois Habitat Trail takes you through three basic types of natural habitat common to this area: tallgrass prairie, marsh, and woodlands. Other trails lead to the Bob Link Arboretum (.75 mile), the Volkening Heritage Farm (.7 mile) and the Ver Merkle Nature Center (.5 mile). The nature trails are not open to bicycles, but there is a rack near the visitor's center. The Nature Center is an earth-sheltered, passive solar museum. It houses exhibits, and a natural history library, and meeting areas. The farm has been restored to approximate an 1880's homestead like one operated by the Boeger family who lived and worked the land here in the 1800's.

The Schaumburg Park District purchased the land in 1982 from Ellsworth Meineke, a Schaumburg resident who recognized the need to preserve part of this rapidly developing suburb. To restore prairies, the district undertook prescribed burn to kill non-native species, and reforested some parts of the preserve to encourage diversity. As a result, you can hear rose-breasted grosbeaks singing their melodious robin-like song in the woods during spring or hear the soft buzzy call of savannah sparrows perched on forbs in the prairie.

Getting There   The Sanctuary is located west of Route 53. Take Meacham Road south to Schaumburg Road, then head west on Schaumburg Road to the Spring Valley Nature Sanctuary main entrance on the south (left) side of the road.

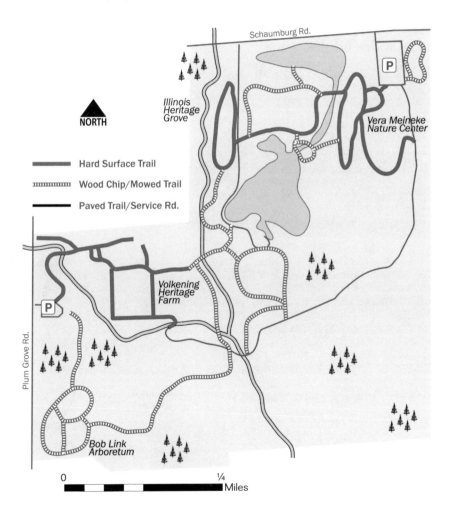

Thorn Creek Forest Preserve

🚲 🏃 🛼 🅰

Trail Length	9.3 miles
Surface	Asphalt
Contact	Forest Preserve District of Cook County 708-366-9420

Thorn Creek Forest Preserve is located in southern Cook County. One section consists of trail through the Sauk Trail lake area and another winds through Lansing Woods and North Creek Meadow. A future extension will link these sections bringing the trail length to 17.5 miles. In addition, from Chicago Heights and as far as Glenwood, there are walks, streets, and informal paths following Thorn Creek but usable only by hikers.

The 10-foot wide paved asphalt Northern Section bike path wanders through open meadows and some woodland areas. The route mostly parallels North Creek as it makes its way west to merge with Thorn Creek on the north side of Glenwood. The trail runs through two other nearby forest preserves with parking area: Lansing Woods Preserve on 183rd Street east of Torrence and Sweet Woods Preserve on Cottage Grove Avenue west of the Calumet Expressway.

East from the North Creek meadow preserve parking area is a pedestrian street crossing at Torrence Avenue, with a trail intersection east of Torrence. The northbound path to the left takes you to the Lansing Woods Preserve at 183th Street. The eastbound path to the right ends north of Lynwood. Back from the North Creek Meadow Preserve, continue west by Glenwood-Lansing road, to a long bridge which provides a safe crossing over the Calumet Expressway. As you approach Cottage Grove Avenue, the path turns north and heads to the Sweet Wood Preserve and Thorn Creek north of Glenwood.

The bike path is well maintained, and the trail is relatively flat with only a few hills in spots. Rustic restrooms, water pumps, and picnic tables are located near the parking areas of the three preserves along the way.

Southern Section. A couple hundred years ago this trail was used as a Native American trade route, running from the Mississippi River to Fort Detroit on Lake St. Clair. Today the Sauk Trail Road in the southern tip of Cook County follows a part of this ancient pathway. Thorton-Lansing Road and Glenwood-Dyer Road follow the crest of sand dunes marking beaches at the southerly limits of Lake Chicago when, during the last glacial period, it stood at levels much higher than present lake Michigan. The Green Lake region has low dunes that were formed in shallow water by wave action during that same glacial period.

Species of trees, shrubs, wildflowers and other plants uncommon in this region exist here because of the unique topography and sandy soil conditions resulting from this geological history. As a side note, Sauk Trail Lake was created by damming Thorn Creek from 26th Street. Wampum Lake was dug to provide earth fill for the Calumet Expressway.

From the parking area entrance at Sauk Trail Woods Grove #6, the trail begins with a lengthy climb through mature woods with little traffic sounds. A side trail to the right leads to 26th Street. Going west the main path crosses over Thorn Creek before it empties into Sauk Lake. West of the lake, the path takes you through several oak groves. There is another side trail to the right leading to the community of Park Forest. The main trail heads back east again crossing Thorn Creek to complete a loop. Take the next path to the right to cross over Sauk Trail Road at the pedestrian crossing. South of Sauk Trail, the trail heads southwest to Steger Road and the Will County line. Along the trail, south of Sauk Trail Road, the home of Revolutionary War veteran John McCoy once stood. The site late became a stop on the "Underground Railway" for former slaves. Leaving the forest preserve, the path continues a short distance along Steger Road. The Section appears generally clean and well-maintained. There are rustic restrooms, picnic tables and a water pump at the Sauk Trail Woods Forest Preserve.

Getting There   **Northern Section** Take the Calumet Expressway to Glenwood-Dyer Road. Head east for .3 miles to Stony Island Avenue. Turn north (left) on Stony Island to Glenwood-Lansing Road, then east (right) on Glenwood-Lansing. Turn left into the North Creek Meadow Preserve parking area. The trail also runs through two other nearby forest preserves with parking areas: Lansing Woods Preserve on 183rd Street east of Torrence and Sweet Woods Preserve on Cottage Grove Avenue west of the Calumet Expressway.

Southern Section Take Sauk Trail Road 1.9 miles west of Dixie Highway to Ashland Avenue. Turn north (right) and proceed .4 mile to Sauk Trail Woods Grove #6 parking area.

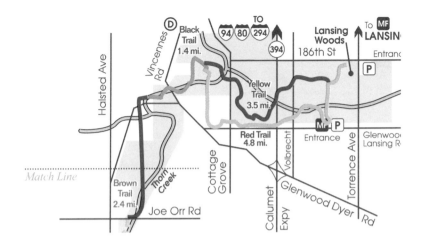

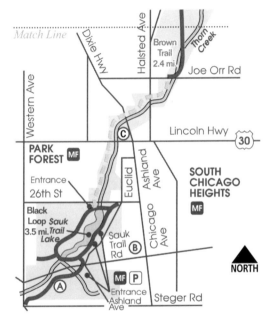

A. Pioneer homesite of John McCoy, soldier in the Revolutionary War; a "station" on the "Underground Railroad" for escaped slaves.

B. Brown's Corners- a crossroads of midwest America in pioneer days-intersection of the Great Sauk Trail with Hubbard's Trace to Danville.

C. Site of Absalom Well's cabin- first white settler in this part of Cook County.

D. Thornton quarry, largest in the Chicago region, is notable for fossils and a coral reef in the Niagara limestone.

Tinley Creek Forest Preserve

Trail Length	23.5 miles
Surface	Asphalt
Information	Forest Preserve District of Cook County 708-366-9420

Tinley Creek Forest Preserve is located in southwestern Cook County. It is situated on a ridge of glacial drift known as the Tinley moraine. This drift, of rocks and other debris, as deposited by the last glacier some 14,000 years ago as it retreated from this area. Northerly and easterly, and much lower, lies the flat Chicago Plain, which was the bed of ancient Lake Chicago and largely swampland until recent times. Southwesterly are low areas known as the "Deep Prairie". Formerly large swamps, they are now drained by Tinley Creek. Following the disappearance of the glacier, its streams eroded deep channels thru the Tinley moraine and meandered across the Chicago Plain until they emptied into Stony Creek, near Blue Island.

Highpoints include an unusual view of the Chicago skyline approximately 20 miles to the northeast, at a high point along 159th Street, just east of Oak Park Avenue. Yankee Woods and St. Mihiel areas are abundant with spring and fall wildflowers, and spectacular autumn color. Small fragments of native prairie containing rare species of plant and insect life also occur in these areas. Blackberry, dewberry and raspberry patches are plentiful in meadows and woodland opening at many locations. Mushrooms can be found in many woodlands during autumn.

Water pumps, picnic tables, and restrooms can be found at the Arrowhead Lake, Turtlehead Lake, Yankee Woods, Midlothian Reservoir and Midlothian Meadows Preserve. You'll find footpaths intersecting with the bike path at the Vollmer Road Preserve, Midlothian Reservoir, and near Tinley Creek south of 143rd Street.

Getting There   There are accesses and parking along Central Avenue between 159th Street and 175th Street in the northern section. Access and parking to the southern loop is available off both Vollmer and Flossmoor Roads. A future extension will link these two sections.

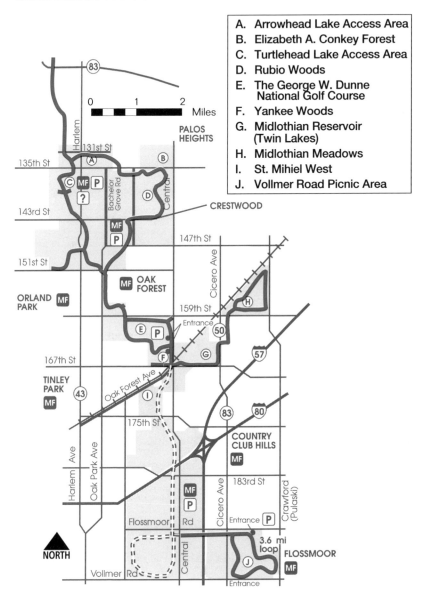

A. Arrowhead Lake Access Area
B. Elizabeth A. Conkey Forest
C. Turtlehead Lake Access Area
D. Rubio Woods
E. The George W. Dunne National Golf Course
F. Yankee Woods
G. Midlothian Reservoir (Twin Lakes)
H. Midlothian Meadows
I. St. Mihiel West
J. Vollmer Road Picnic Area

Tri-County State Park

Trail Length	4 miles
Surface	Limestone screenings
Information	Forest Preserve District of DuPage County 630-933-7200

Tri-County State Park encompasses 501 acres of open space that extends into DuPage, Kane and Cook counties. The park is owned by the Illinois Dept. of Natural Resources and managed by the Forest Preserve District of DuPage County, and was opened to the public in April of 2003. The park was once mainly wet, tallgrass prairie, but once settled by Europeans, was mostly used for agricultural purposes until its acquisition by the Illinois DNR in 1989. The Visitor Center provides a window into the park's restoration with photomurals, interactive displays and theater videos. A picnic area and drinking water are available.

The 1.5 mile Bluestem Trail circles the marsh and the Land and Water Reserve and visits the point where the three counties meet. There is a short trail spur providing an overlook of the marsh. The 1.5 mile Blazing Star Trail follows the edge of the flood plain and the north boundary of the park past a housing development. It includes a connector trail from the Bluestem Trail. The .7 mile Indigo Trail traces the south edge of the creek and is a quick hike from the picnic area. There is also a connector trail that links the Indigo and Bluestem trails and crosses Brewster Creek by bridge.

Getting There   The main entrance is located on the north side of Stearns Road west of Powis Road in Barlett. The park is open daily from one hour after sunrise to one hour after sunset.

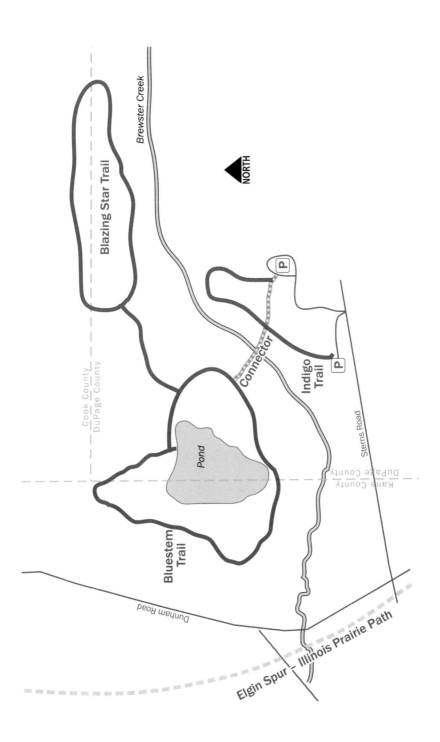

Brewster Creek

NORTH

Blazing Star Trail

Cook County
DuPage County

Connector

Indigo Trail

P

P

Sterns Road

Pond

Kane County
DuPage County

Bluestem Trail

Dunham Road

Elgin Spur — Illinois Prairie Path

Wolf Road Prairie

Trail Length	2 miles
Surface	1.5 miles sidewalk, .5 miles mowed turf
Information	Forest Preserve District of Cook County 708-771-1330

Wolf Road Prairie is an excellent example of the original tallgrass prairie of Illinois and is the largest prairie of its type remaining in the Chicago area. It is recognized as the finest and largest silt loam soil prairie east of the Mississippi River, and it is incredibly diverse. The prairie is dominated by big bluestem, little bluestem, prairie dropseed and Indian grass. A marsh dominated by bulrush and cattail and a small savanna remnant also occur here. The savanna is dominated by bur oak with wild hyacinth, groundnut and meadow rue beneath the trees. Western chorus frog, fox snake, common snipe and swamp sparrow are some of the animals that occupy this preserve.

In the 1920s, developers obtained this 80 acre site for residential development. It was the Great Depression that brought this development plan to a halt. Also the wetlands here made the site ill-suited for growing crops or grazing animals. Today the only surviving "development" is a grid of paired sidewalks that crisscross the southern half of the preserve.

You'll find no facilities here, so bring your own water. The Wolf Road Prairie is preserved by a consortium consisting of an active volunteer group called Save the Prairie Society, the Illinois Dept. of Natural Resources, the Forest Preserve District of Cook County, and the Illinois

Nature Preserves Commission. Monthly Ecotours and special events are held throughout the year covering various conservation topics.

Getting There Take Ogden Avenue east of I-294 past Bemis Woods Forest Preserve to Wolf Road. Head north on Wolf Road to 31st Street, then west (left) on 31st Street for .1 mile. There are three small concrete parking areas north of 31st Street. The pathway near the entrance is a set of rectangular grids of concrete connected with narrow earthen footpaths. The path to the right takes you to an information signpost and a 260-year old bur oak tree. The tree serves as an excellent example of its species whole thick, resilient bark survived the frequent fires that swept through and rejuvenated the area.

White Oak

Interconnecting Trails
Des Plaines River Trail and Greenway

Trail Length	33 miles (49 miles with loops)
Surface	Limestone screenings
Contact	Lake County Forest Preserves 847-367-6640

The Des Plaines River Greenway covers more than 7,700 acres and protects land along more than 85 percent of the river in Lake County, providing wildlife habitat, flood protection and recreation opportunities.

The multi-use, 31 mile trail connects 10 Forest Preserves and ties in over 100 miles of trails. The bridges and underpasses allow continuous travel from Wadsworth Road to Half Day Road (Route 22) without crossing any major roads. Road crossings are necessary north of Wadsworth Road and south of Half Day Road. The Des Plaines River Trail is open to hiking, biking, cross-country skiing, horseback riding, and snowmobiling (north of Independence Grove in Libertyville only). At the intersections, signs indicate which uses are allowed on the other local trails. This trail is just one leg of a whole trail network that includes the North Shore Bike Path, the McClory Trail and the Millennium Trail.

The trail provides access to a 1.2 mile asphalt paved community path along the north side of Washington Street running between Milwaukee Avenue and a little west of O'Plaine Road. The short .2 mile eastbound path that you'll see south of Washington Street and a large retention pond exits on a street providing entrance to the Gurnee Water Works entrance. The North Shore Bike Path can be accessed at the Route 176 underpass. There is also the accessible east/west Lincolnshire Civic Center Path that runs along Route 22.

In northern Lake County, open areas such as prairies and savannas are common, the valley is wide and the river meanders. In southern Lake County, the river running through the valley is narrow and it runs a straighter course. You'll also see more woodland with oaks, hickories and maples.

In times past, the river would often block wildfires that would rage from west Lake County. Thus to the west of the river, prairies, savannas, and oaks, which can withstand fire are common, while maples, which cannot withstand fire, are found on the east bank of the river. The lowlands of the Greenway provide a natural benefit by reducing damage from heavy rains and snowmelt entering the river. It not only stores water, it cleanses it too. Located south of Wadsworth Road is the 550 acre Wetlands Research Project. This project undertakes large-scale research, wetland construction and management.

Getting There   As indicated on the following map, there are numerous access points and parking areas along the entire trail. Open hours are 6:30 am to sunset.

Des Plaines River Trail and Greenway (continued)

Northern Section

Road Crossings – North To South

Route 173 – road crossing, no light

Wadsworth Road – road crossing, no light

Route 132 (Grand Avenue) – underpass

Washington Street – underpass

I-94 - underpass

Route 137 – underpass

Oak Spring Road – road crossing, no light

Route 176 – underpass

Old Rockland Road – road crossing, no light

St. Mary's Road – underpass

Old School Road – road crossing, no light

St. Mary's Road – underpass

Route 60 – underpass

Route 22 - underpass

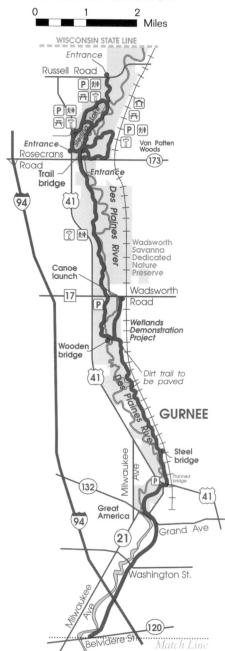

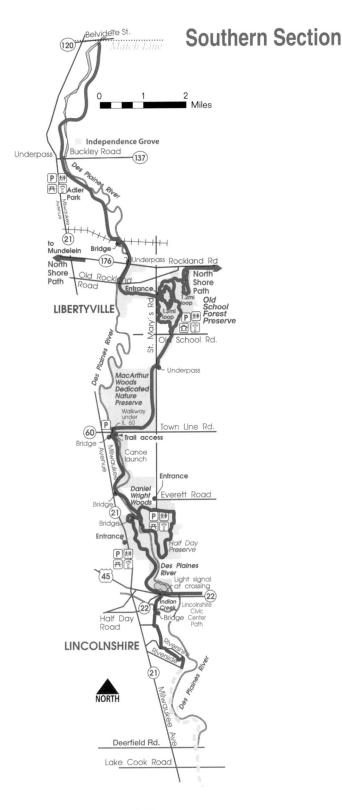

Belvidere St.
120
Match Line

0 1 2 Miles

Independence Grove
Buckley Road
137

Underpass

Des Plaines River

P
Adler
Park

Milwaukee Avenue

to
Mundelein
21

Bridge
176
Underpass Rockland Rd.

North
Shore
Path

Old Rockland
Road

Entrance

LIBERTYVILLE

North
Shore
Path

1.2mi
loop

Old
School
Forest
Preserve

1.3mi
loop

P

St. Mary's Rd.

Old School Rd.

Underpass

Des Plaines River

*MacArthur
Woods
Dedicated
Nature
Preserve*

Walkway
under
IL 60

P

60

Bridge

Town Line Rd.

Trail access

Canoe
launch

Milwaukee Avenue

Entrance

*Daniel
Wright
Woods*

Everett Road

Bridge
21

P

Bridge

Entrance

P

*Half Day
Preserve*

45

*Des Plaines
River*

Light signal
at crossing

22

22

*Indian
Creek*

Lincolnshire
Civic
Center
Path

Half Day
Road

Bridge

LINCOLNSHIRE

Rivershire

Riverside

Des Plaines River

21

NORTH

Milwaukee Ave.

Deerfield Rd.

Lake Cook Road

Find me a place, safe and serene,

away from the terror I see on the screen.

A place where my soul can find some peace,

away from the stress and the pressures released.

A corridor of green not far from my home

for fresh air and exercise, quiet will roam.

Summer has smells that tickle my nose

and fall has the leaves that crunch under my toes.

Beware, comes a person we pass in a while

with a wave and hello and a wide friendly smile.

Recreation trails are the place to be,

to find that safe haven of peace and serenity.

By Beverly Moore, Illinois Trails Conservancy

Interconnecting Trails
Grand Illinois Trail

Trail Length	475 miles
Surface	Varies
Information	Illinois Dept. of Conservation 217-782-3715

The Grand Illinois Trail forms a circular loop from Navy Pier in Chicago past Starved Rock State park to the Mississippi River via the I&M Canal State Trail, the Kaskaskia-Alliance Trail and the Hennepin Canal State Trail. The trail then heads north along the Great River Trail to Savanna and Mississippi Palisades State Park, continues along the to Galena then returns to Chicago through other counties bordering Wisconsin.

The Grand Illinois Trail system will eventually contain over 500 miles of rail trails, bike paths, canal towpaths, and greenways along with street routes and lightly traveled town and county roads as it traverses the state. Camping and lodging is available along the way. Trail enthusiasts will be able to enjoy nearby adventure vacations taking on the entire trail in a single effort or more likely completing one segment at a time. In addition to the trails described in this guidebook, the Grand Illinois Trails includes parts of the Fox River Trail, the Illinois Prairie Path, the Prairie Trail, the Des Plaines River Trail, the Robert McClory and Green Bay Trails, and other existing and planned on-and off-road routes.

The Grand Illinois will connect with a national path system, also under development, the 6,300 mile American Discovery Trail. From the trailhead near the Atlantic Ocean at the Cape Henlopen State Park in

Delaware to the Pacific Ocean at the Point Reyes National Seashore in California, the American Discovery Trail will run through urban and remote areas in 15 states and Washington D.C. Through the Midwestern states including Illinois, there will be both a northern and a southern route forming a gigantic 2,500 mile loop from Cincinnati to Denver. It will connect to six national scenic trails and ten national historic trails as well as many regional and local trails systems. You can contact the American Discovery Trail Society at 800-663-2387 for more information.

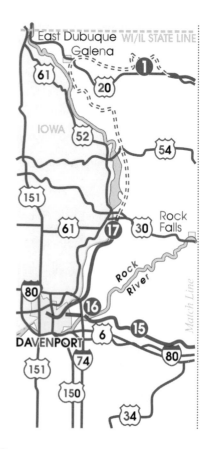

GRAND ILLINOIS TRAIL SYSTEM SEGMENTS

1. Local roads
2. Pecatonica Trail
3. Rockford Area Trails
4. Stone Bridge and Long Prairie Trails
5. Conceptual connection
6. Crystal Lake/Harvard Trail segment
7. Prairie Trail segment
8. Fox River Trail segment
9. Illinois Prairie Path segment
10. Des Plaines River Trail segment
11. Centennial Trail
12. Lockport Historical & Joliet Heritage Trails (& roads)
13. Illinois and Michigan (I & M) Canal State Trail segment
14. Conceptual connection
15. Hennepin Canal State Trail segment
16. Conceptual connection
17. Great River Trail

Interconnecting Trails
I&M Canal National Historic Corridor

The opening of the Illinois & Michigan Canal ushered in a new era in trade and travel for the nation. By connecting the waters of the Illinois River with those of Lake Michigan (hence the name, hereafter referred to as the I&M Canal), the canal created an all-water route from New York to New Orleans, with Chicago as the crucial mid-point. The I&M Canal, opened 23 years after the Erie Canal, was the last of the great U. S. shipping canals of the nineteenth century. Following up on the Erie's success, the I&M was the final link in a chain of waterways that helped fuel the nation's economic growth.

In 1673, Louis Jolliet and Father Jacques Marquette, were the first Europeans to venture into the area. They and their company were returning to Canada from their explorations down the Mississippi River.

Marquette and Jolliet had traveled north from the Mississippi by way of the Illinois and Des Plaines Rivers. At a point now known as the Chicago Portage, they encountered a low divide that separated them from the Chicago River and Lake Michigan. Jolliet early on saw the opportunity of providing an uninterrupted route to the Gulf of Mexico. He wrote that if a short canal were dug through the portage, one could travel from Lake Michigan to the Gulf entirely by boat.

The French continued to control the region until their defeat by the British in the French and Indian War. After the American Revolution, the American government negotiated a treaty with the Pottawatomie tribe, in which the Pottawatomie ceded six square miles of land at the mouth of the Chicago River. Part of this area became the site of Fort Dearborn.

Interest in a canal began to increase in the early 1800's, and in 1816, the Pottawatomie ceded land ten miles on either side of the Des Plaines and Illinois Rivers from Lake Michigan to the Fox River. In 1823 Illinois created a Canal Commission, but progress was limited by the lack of financial resources. In 1835 a new Canal Commission was formed and, unlike the first, it was empowered to raise money.

The Commission had a federal grant of 284,000 acres of land along the proposed canal route, which it tried to sell for $1.25 an acre to fund construction. Land sales were difficult, but enough funds were raised to start canal construction on Independence Day, 1836. Construction proceeded stop-and-go, but after a four-year stoppage, new funding was secured from English and eastern investors and the Illinois and Michigan Canal was officially opened its locks in 1848.

Chief Engineer William Gooding was put in charge of engineering and construction. His plan divided the Canal into three sections: The Summit segment (Chicago to Lockport), the Middle segment (Lockport to Seneca), and the Western segment (Seneca to LaSalle). The Canal was to be 60 feet wide at water level, 36 feet wide at the bottom, and six feet deep along its entire 96 mile length. The Canal connected to Lake Michigan via 4.5 miles of the Chicago River. A total of 17 locks were built on the Canal. These locks were needed to lift or lower boats

I&M Canal National Historic Corridor (continued)

along the course of the Canal as water levels changes. Other construction included aqueducts to carry the Canal over rivers and streams, bridges, dams, lockkeepers' houses and the towpath along which mules pulled the canal boats.

For the first time, a cargo of sugar and other goods from New Orleans reached the docks of Buffalo, New York in April of 1848. From a trickle, the commerce between east and west swelled into a continuous flow of people and goods. Chicago became the Midwest's hub, and the city's population soared 600% in the decade after the opening of the Canal. The Chicago and Rock Island Railroad paralleled the canal by 1853 and took away the canal passenger trade. The canal held its own in competing with the railroads in the shipment of freight. Tolls reached a peak of over $300,000 in 1866, and tonnage topped out at over 1 million tons in 1881. The Canal's intense growth began to wane by the late 1880s, and beginning in 1871 the I&M carried sewage away from Chicago.

In 1900, the larger Sanitary and Ship Canal began operating, carrying both wastes and larger, more modern barges. All use of the I&M Canal ended in 1933, with the opening of the Canal's modern successor – the Illinois Waterway.

On August 24, 1984, President Ronald Reagan signed legislation establishing the region as the nation's first National Heritage Corridor. The I&M Canal National Heritage Corridor is a 100 mile long cultural park between Chicago and LaSalle/Peru. It contains roughly 322,000 acres within the counties of Cook, DuPage, Will, Grundy and LaSalle.

CANAL CORRIDOR ASSOCIATION

The Canal Corridor Association (CCA) is a nonprofit membership organization that creates destinations for learning and fun throughout the Illinois & Michigan Canal National Heritage Corridor. The 65+ miles of recreational trails in the Heritage Corridor are among its most popular features. CCA is installing mile markers that feature tidbits of canal history, along with life-size sculptures of canal pioneers along the Heritage Corridor's trails to bring the early days of the historic, hand-dug canal to life. CCA also works with partners along the Heritage Corridor to create parks, protect nature and preserve history for visitors to enjoy. Visit www.canalcor.org to learn more about CCA and become a member.

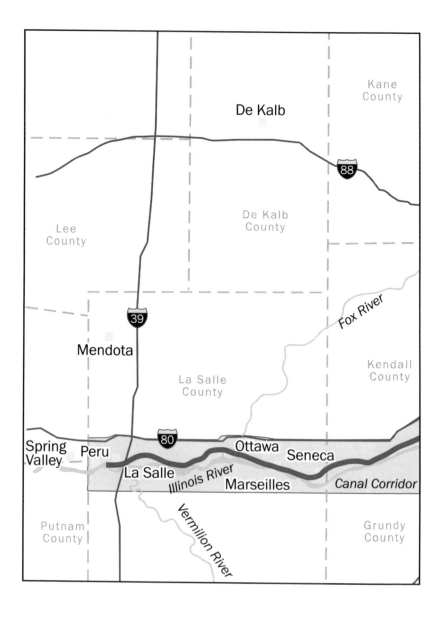

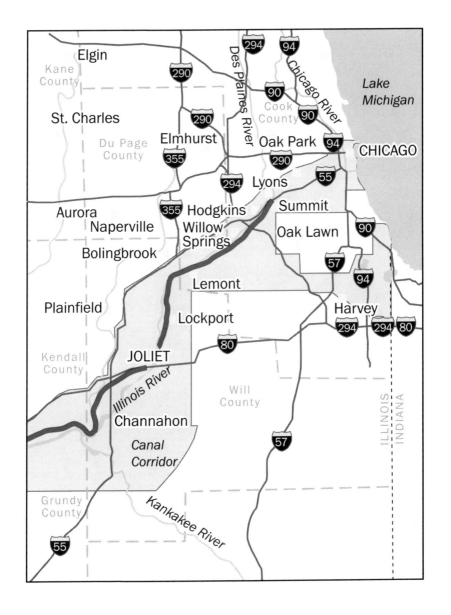

Interconnecting Trails
Robert McClory Bike Path

Trail Length	25 miles
Surface	Limestone screening, paved
Contact	Lake County Division of Transportation 847-362-3950

The Robert McClory Bike Path serves as a continuation of the Green Bay Trail. It is built on the Lake County portion of the abandoned Chicago North Shore Milwaukee Railway right-of-way. The path runs for 25 miles from the Cook County line at Lake Cook Road to the Wisconsin border. South of the Lake County line the trail continues as the Green Bay Trail into Kenilworth. North of Lake County into Wisconsin it continues as the Kenosha County Trail. It also connects to the North Shore Trail in Lake Bluff and the Zion Bike Path. The trail generally parallels the east side of Green Bay Road and the west side of Sheridan Road.

The mostly urban to suburban setting of this ride provides ample opportunities to enjoy the many eating establishments and beautiful homes. It's open to bicycling, hiker/joggers, in-line skaters and cross-country skiing. Between Cook County and Lake Bluff, the trail is limestone screening to Highland Park and paved north of Highwood to Lake Bluff's city limits. North of Lake Bluff to Wisconsin the surface is mostly limestone screenings except for a 1 mile concrete sidewalk section in North Chicago and a 1.5 mile asphalt paved section that forms the west side of the Zion Bike Path loop.

The Robert McClory trail officially begins northbound from Lake Cook Road, a little east of Green Bay Road, by the Braeside train station. The surface here is crushed gravel. A mile north of this point you'll come to the Ravinia train station, with restaurants nearby. There is parking at the Ravinia Festival Park south lot on St. John's Avenue in Highland Park. Note that cars left after 4 pm in the summer during the concert season will be ticketed. For a short side trip go to Rosewood Beach Park with its scenic view on a high bluff overlooking Lake Michigan. To get there head east on Roger Williams Avenue for ¾ miles, past Jens Jensen Park.

There are several sidewalk & street connections as you proceed north through Highland Park and Highwood. The off-road temporarily ends at the Highland Park train station at the intersection of St. John's and Laurel Avenues. To continue north, take St. John's one block north to Central Avenue. Turn east (right) a block to Sheridan Road. Turn north (left) on Sheridan pass Moraine Park, where you'll find drinking water, restrooms, and a picnic area. Pick up Sheridan Road again by following the signs north into Highwood by way of Edgecliff Drive, Oak Street, and Walker Avenue. You'll pass Fort Sheridan on the east. Continue north along Sheridan Road to the Fort Sheridan train station at the intersection of Old Elm road and Sheridan Road north of Highwood, where the trail picks up again, and is asphalt surfaced. The distance of this described trail gap is about 3 miles.

As you continue north into Lake Forest, you'll pass DePaul's University Barat College and through the downtown area. Here there are a number of good restaurants, an ice cream shop and many shopping opportunities.

Market Square, built in 1916, was the first shopping area in the County. If you turn east (right) on Deerpath Road for 1 mile, it will take you to Forest Park and the scenic bluffs overlooking Lake Michigan. There are bike racks by the stairs to the beach, and a long elevated boardwalk that winds through the trees to the shoreline.

There are two intersections on the trail before you cross over the bridge to the Lake Bluff train station. The Robert McClory Path continues north. The two westbound intersections take you on the North Shore Path, which parallels the south side of Route 176. There is parking in downtown Lake Bluff near the train station, at Sheridan Road and Scranton. From the train station, the trees provide a canopy of shade during the summer.

In North Chicago you pass the Great Lakes Naval Training Center on the right, and you'll come to another street connection. At Martin Luther King Drive (22nd Street), go west one block to Commonwealth, then north a block to Broadway. A short distance to the right you pick up the trail again at Boak Park, just west of Glen. There are many street crossings as you proceed through North Chicago and Waukegan. You can park your car on one of the side streets near the Lake County YMCA on Golf Avenue for easy trail access in Waukegan. From Golf Avenue for the 3.5 miles to Zion there are only three street crossings. The setting in this stretch is quiet and suburban, with scrub growth and low trees lining the trail.

As you enter Zion, the trail is paved. Just north of 21st Street the crushed gravel path resumes at the trail intersection. Stay left as the Zion Bike Path goes to the right. For a detour to the Illinois Beach State Park, go east on Carmel Blvd at the southwest corner of the Zion Bike Path for a mile to Sheridan Road. Cross Sheridan Road, looping north to Shiloh Blvd. Just past Shiloh is a path leading to the Northern Unit of the Illinois Beach State Park.

North of Zion the setting becomes more rural, with woods with meadows bordering the trail. As you cross into Wisconsin past the Russell Road overpass, the path continues for another 3.5 miles as the Kenosha County Bike Trail. The setting along this stretch is mostly rural. At 89th Street the off-road trail ends. There is a convenient place to rest across the street at Anderson Park.

If you decide to continue on and explore Kenosha's parks and the harbor along Lake Michigan, take 89th Street east to 17th Avenue, then south to 91st Street. Go East on 91st Street to 7th Avenue, then north to Southport Park. Sightseeing as you continue north includes the Third Avenue Historic District. This is Kenosha's 'mansion' district with many large period revival homes. Further north is Eichelman Park, which has a bathing beach, and Kenosha Marina, a large boat slip marina with entertainment and recreation facilities.

Backtracking to where we started at Lake Cook Road, you can take the connecting 6 mile, paved Green Bay Trail south to Forest Avenue in Kenilworth where it ends. One way to get from there to the Chicago Lakefront Bike Path is to take Forest Avenue east to Sheridan Road, then

Robert McClory Bike Path (continued)

Sheridan Road south to Lincoln Avenue in Evanston. You'll find the Lakefront Path trailhead east of Sheridan Road off Lincoln Avenue.

Getting There   There are multiple accesses to the path throughout the length of the path. Some of the locations for off street parking are described above.

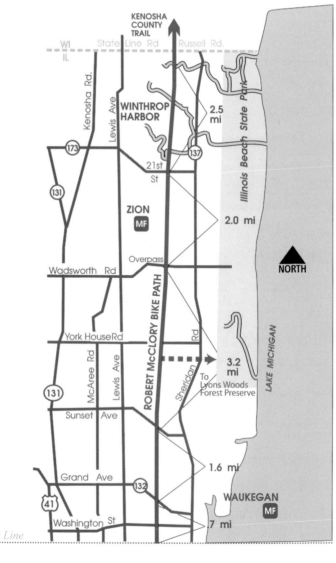

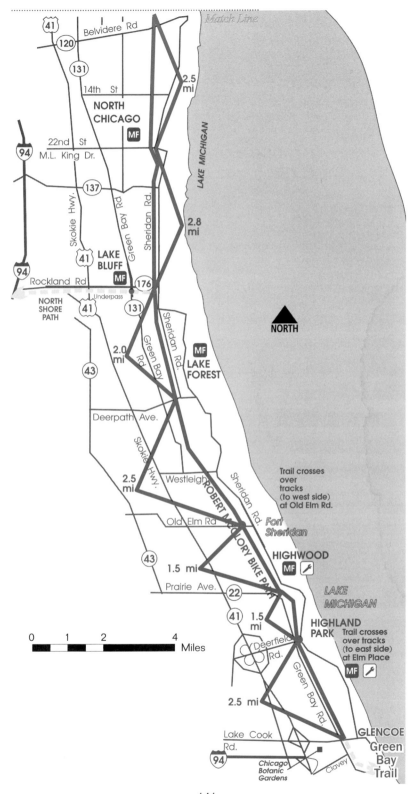

Organizations

Bicycling

Chicagoland Bicycle Federation
650 S. Clark Street
Chicago, IL 60605
312-427-3325

League of Illinois Bicyclists
1550 Cheshire Dr.
Aurora, IL 60504
530-978-0583

RIDE
Recreation for Individuals Dedicated
to the Environment
208 S. La Salle Street, Suite 1700
Chicago, IL 60604
312-853-2820

Hiking

American Hiking Society
1422 Fenwick Lane
Silver Spring, MI 20910
800-972-8608

Forest Trails Hiking Club
630-262-1868

Environmental

Forest Preserve District of Cook
County
536 North Harlem Avenue
River Forest, IL 60305
708-366-9420
fpdcc.org

Illinois Trails Conservancy
PO Box 10, 144 W. Main Street
Capron, IL 61012
815-569-2472

Illinois Dept of Natural Resources
(DNR)
One Natural Resources Way
Springfield, IL 62702
217-782-6302

Friends of the Chicago River
407 S. Dearborn , suite 1580
Chicago, IL 60605
312-939-0490

Friends of the Lake Katherine
Nature Preserve
7402 Lake Katherine Drive
Palos Heights, IL 60463
708-361-1873

Friend of the Parks
55 E. Washington, Suite 911
Chicago, IL 60605
312-857-2757

Illinois Audubon Society
PO Box 2418
Danville, IL 61834
217-446-5085

Illinois Ornithological Society
PO Box 931
Lake Forest, IL 60045

The Nature Conservancy
Illinois Field Office
Volunteer Stewardship Office
8 S. Michigan, Suite 900
Chicago, IL 60603
312-580-2100

Save the Prairie Society
10327 Elizabeth
Westchester, IL 60154
708-865-8730

Sierra Club-Illinois Chapter
200 N Michigan, Suite 505
Chicago, IL 60612
312-251-1680

Canal Corridor Association
Dedicated to community economic
development, historic preservation
and conservation within the Heritage
Corridor.
www.canalcor.org

Friends of the I&M Canal National
Heritage Corridor
Dedicated to the preservation of
the I&M Canal by promoting its
maintenance and history.
630-324-1528

Heritage Corridor Convention &
Visitors Bureau
Publishes a visitor's guide, and
packages overnight tours.
815-727-2323
www.heritagecorridorcvb.com

Bicycle Clubs

Arlington Hgts. Bicycle Association
847-225-3468

Chicago Area Mountain Bikers
708-749-8488
atb@cambr.org

Chicago Cycling Club
773-509-8093

Chicago Heartland Cycling Club
773-465-8005
fatback@aol.com

Elmhurst Bicycling Club
630-415-BIKE

Evanston Bicycle Club
847-604-1225
evbike@evanstonbikeclub.org

Mr. Prospect Bicycle Club
Des Plaines
847-439-9737

North Branch Cycling Club
Chicago
rsliwinski@cbbel.com

Northbrook Bicycle Club
847-419-3635
riderf@hotmail.com

Pedal Pushers
Wheaton
630-665-1415

Schaumburg Bike Club
847-622-5356
schaumburgbikeclub@aol.com

Wheeling Wheelmen
Buffalo Grove
847-520-5010
wheeling@wheelmen.com

Windy City Cycling Club
Chicago
info@windycyclingclub.com

Points of Interest

Adler Planetarium and Astronomy
Museum
1300 S. Lake Shore Drive
312-322-9444

Argonne National Laboratory
9700 S. Cass Avenue
Argonne
630-252-2000

Brookfield Zoo
1st Avenue at 31st Street
Brookfield
708-485-0263

Field Museum of Natural History
1200 S. Lake Shore Drive
Chicago
312-343-5354

General Fry's Landing
Stephen and River Streets
Lemont
630-243-2700

Lincoln Park Zoo
2001 N. Clark St.
Chicago, IL 60614
312-742-2000

Little Red Schoolhouse Nature
Center
104th Avenue between 95th & 107th
Willow Springs
708-839-6897

Museum of Science & Industry
5700 S. Lake Shore Drive
Chicago
312-684-1414

Shedd Aquarium
1200 S. Lake Shore Drive
Chicago
312-939-2438

American Bike Trails publishes
and distributes
maps, books and guides for the bicyclist.

For more information:
www.abtrails.com